FROM THE DEEP WOODS
TO CIVILIZATION

Charles Alexander Eastman
(Ohiyesa)

FROM THE DEEP WOODS
TO CIVILIZATION

CHAPTERS IN THE AUTOBIOGRAPHY
OF AN INDIAN

BY
CHARLES A. EASTMAN
(OHIYESA)

INTRODUCTION BY
Raymond Wilson

University of Nebraska Press
Lincoln and London

First Bison Book printing: 1977
Most recent printing indicated by first digit below:

             7   8   9   10

Library of Congress Cataloging in Publication Data

Eastman, Charles Alexander, 1858–1939.
  From the deep woods to civilization.

  Reprint of the 1936 ed. published by Little,
Brown, Boston.
    1. Eastman, Charles Alexander, 1858–1939.
2. Santee Indians—Biography. I. Title.
E99.S22E183   1977   970'.004'97 [B]   77–7226
ISBN 0–8032–0936–3
ISBN 0–8032–5873–9 pbk.

Published by arrangement with Eleanor E. Mensel and
Virginia E. Whitbeck.

⊖

Manufactured in the United States of America

INTRODUCTION

*The North American Indian was the highest
type of pagan and uncivilized man. He pos-
sessed not only a superb physique but a remarkable mind. But the Indian no longer
exists as a natural and free man. Those rem-
nants which now dwell upon the reservations
present only a sort of tableau—a fictitious
copy of the past.*
                    Charles A. Eastman,
                    Indian Boyhood, p.v.

When first published in 1916, *From the
Deep Woods to Civilization* received largely
favorable reviews. Only the critic for the
Nation found the book tiresome and its author
morbidly fascinated by cultural decay. Most
reviewers considered it an evocative, gracious-
ly written testament of one Indian's remarkable
adaptation to the white man's world.[1]

Although considered by many to be a full-
blood Sioux, a claim which he himself never
made, Charles Alexander Eastman (Ohiyesa)

v

was, in fact, a mixed-blood. His maternal
grandfather was Captain Seth Eastman, a famous western artist. In the 1830s, while sta-
tioned at Fort Snelling near the present-day
site of Saint Paul, Minnesota, Captain Eastman
took as his wife a daughter of Chief Cloudman
of the Mdewakanton Sioux. Their union produced Mary Nancy Eastman, who in 1847 wed
Many Lightnings, a Wahpeton Sioux. They
had five children—four boys and a girl. Soon
after the birth of her last child, a son, in 1858,
Mary Eastman died. The infant received the
name Hakadah ("the Pitiful Last"). Many
Lightnings's mother assumed responsibility for
him. Four years later, in celebration of a
victory by his band over another in a lacrosse
game, the child was awarded the name
Ohiyesa ("the Winner").[2]

The two decades following Ohiyesa's birth
were filled with dramatic changes for the
Santee (Eastern) division of the Sioux, which
included the Mdewakantons and Wahpetons.
Consigned to a reservation in Minnesota some
years before, and driven by destitution, starva-
tion, and goverment fraud, the Santees re-
belled in 1862. It was during this Sioux Uprising that Ohiyesa was separated from his father.
Believing that Many Lightnings had been

killed by soldiers sent to crush the insurrection, Ohiyesa's grandmother and uncle fled to Canada with the child. There Ohiyesa was raised to become a successful warrior and hunter—and to hate white Americans because of his father's death, which he must avenge.

When Ohiyesa was fifteen and ready "to be initiated into the ritual of the war-path," his life was dramatically interrupted by the reappearance of his father, who had been converted to Christianity while serving a prison sentence for his involvement in the uprising, and had come to take his son back to his homestead in Dakota Territory. In *Indian Boyhood*, Eastman would later affectionately recall his childhood days in Canada and the traditional Sioux way of life—a life-style which no longer existed when the book was published in 1902.³ In *From the Deep Woods to Civilization*, he continues the narrative, recounting his initiation into the white world and his subsequent role as mediator between two often conflicting cultures.

A journeyman in the white world, Eastman learned to read and write English, became a Christian, obtained a medical degree, and, at the age of thirty-two, decided to put his education and training to good use by returning to

his people in 1890 as government physician at
Pine Ridge Agency, South Dakota. This was
the first of several positions he held as an
employee of the Bureau of Indian Affairs.

Indian temper at Pine Ridge had almost
reached the breaking point when Eastman arrived. The Sioux, who had suffered many injustices at the government's hands, hoped that
their adoption of the Ghost Dance religion
would rid them of the white man and his institutions forever and bring back the old ways of
life. Eastman was an eyewitness to the events
leading up to the confrontation at Wounded
Knee, and his account, often employed by
present-day students of the tragedy, is considered accurate.

In his discussion of the embroilment between himself and Captain George Le Roy
Brown, Indian agent at Pine Ridge, Eastman is
somewhat less objective. Correspondence on
this matter in the National Archives and the
Indian Rights Association Papers reveals that
the controversy was far more complicated and
confusing than Eastman suggests. There certainly existed a personality conflict between
the two men, and many of the charges and
countercharges were neither substantiated nor
refuted. Profoundly disillusioned with the

whole affair, Eastman, who had been offered transfers to other agencies, preferred to tender his resignation.

Eastman later held four other positions as a BIA employee. Although he does not mention it in *From the Deep Woods*, he served as outing agent at Carlisle Indian School in Pennsylvania from 1899 to 1900 and as government physician at Crow Creek Agency, South Dakota, from 1900 to 1903. At Carlisle he shared a strong rapport with Major Richard H. Pratt, the school's superintendent, but his tenure at Crow Creek was less congenial. Once again he became involved in a controversy with an agent. It was not on the same scale as the one at Pine Ridge, however, and he left to accept the job of revising the Sioux allotment rolls, which he labored on from 1903 to 1909.

Although Eastman worked as a BIA employee, he frequently pointed to the Bureau's ineffectiveness and demanded that it be abolished. In its place he suggested forming a commission, with at least half of its members Indian. This commission would have direct authority to handle Indian matters and would not be subject to political pressures.[4] Many people today continue to support similar programs.

Introduction

Besides service to his people as a government official, Eastman's greatest impact and contributions in aid of Indians came through his writings and subsequent lecture tours. His eleven books—among them *Old Indian Days* (1907), *The Soul of the Indian* (1911), *The Indian Today* (1915), and *Indian Heroes and Great Chieftains* (1918)—and numerous articles attempted to correct misapprehensions whites had about Indians and to bring the two races closer together. In all of his published works, his wife, Elaine Goodale Eastman, served as his editorial collaborator. He tried to convey the same message through his speaking engagements, which took him throughout the United States and to England on two separate occasions.

Eastman helped found the Society of American Indians, a pan-Indian organization, in 1911, and worked with other educated Indians such as Arthur C. Parker, Thomas L. Sloan, and Henry Roe Cloud to improve conditions among their people. He supported programs calling for better health care and educational opportunities for Indians. Especially on two of the major issues of the early twentieth century affecting Indians, Eastman expressed definite views. He fervently supported Indian citizenship and pointed to Indians' participation as American soldiers in World War I as an example of why it should immediately be granted. The peyote question, however, was another matter. He considered peyote a dangerous drug and thought it should not be a part of any religious ceremony.[5]

In 1921, Eastman and his wife separated after thirty years of marriage. Two years later Eastman reentered the government service as an Indian inspector and served until 1925. He was also selected in 1923 as a member of Secretary of the Interior Herbert W. Work's Committee of One Hundred, organized to study federal Indian policy.[6]

During the 1930s Eastman spent a great deal of time in semiretirement at a cabin he had purchased in Desbarats, Ontario. This solitary existence, communing with nature, brought back memories of his childhood days. He enjoyed rising early and going hunting and fishing. Occasionally he accepted a lecture engagement, and he was preparing a major study of the Sioux nation, which, unfortunately, he never completed. On September 22, 1933, at the Chicago World's Fair, the Indian Council Fire, another pan-Indian organization, presented a medal honoring the most distin-

guished achievements by an American Indian.
From more than fifty people considered for the
award, the committee chose Charles Eastman.
On January 8, 1939, after a career almost
totally devoted to helping his race, Eastman
died at the age of eighty.

Apart from its intrinsic interest, Eastman's
autobiography is remarkable as a social and
historical document. As an educated Indian
and author, Eastman was a rarity. His assimilation and acculturation had been unique.
Both cultures accepted him, and, in turn, he
tried to get them to accept each other. The
inner pressures and conflicts which he faced
must have been tremendous. Although he
never advised Indians to abandon their her-
itage, Eastman, like others of the small group
of educated Indians, urged them to accept the
positive aspects of white society which would
benefit them. Obtaining a proper education
was paramount. His views on the compatibility
of Christianity and Indian religious training are
controversial, yet they demonstrate how he
personally reconciled this apparent incon-
gruity.

Eastman's life, especially his education, was
offered by contemporary reform-minded Americans as proof of the Indians' capacity to

become assimilated by white, middle-class America. He had many friends among the advocates of Indian reform, particularly in Boston, a center of humanitarian activity. The Indian reformers included, among other groups, the Board of Indian Commissioners, appointed by the government to investigate Indian matters and make recommendations on policy, and the Lake Mohonk Conferences of Friends of the Indian, held annually in New York to discuss Indian affairs. These organizations supported assimilation as the solution to the so-called Indian problem.

More a faith than a practical program, Indian assimilation centered on the transformation of the savage into citizen. Education was the path that led from the wilderness to civilization. Charles Eastman symbolized the adaptability of the American Indian. Prominent Indian reformers and humanitarians constantly cited Eastman as the classic example of what an Indian could achieve. Among those who held him in high esteem were the Reverend Alfred L. Riggs, superintendent of Santee Indian School; Commissioner of Indian Affairs Thomas J. Morgan; Professor Warren K. Moorehead, a member of the Board of Indian Commissioners; Albert K. Smiley, founder of

Introduction

the Lake Mohonk Conference of Friends of the Indian; and Frank Wood, a Bostonian who had a profound interest in helping Indians and whom Eastman considered his white father. Yet unlike many of these reformers, who were quick to excoriate Indian civilization, Eastman fiercely retained an almost spiritual identification with his own race.

It should also be remembered that Eastman was writing for a white audience, and even though he made some bold and critical statements regarding the bad aspects of white civilization, especially in *From the Deep Woods to Civilization*, he chose his words carefully. Neither a militant nor (in today's jargon) an "Uncle Tomahawk" or "apple," Eastman was a major figure directly involved with helping his fellow Indians adapt to white culture and at the same time retain their Indian identity. *From the Deep Woods to Civilization* and Eastman's other works are valuable sources for the study of Native American history. Fully aware of the gross injustices that Indians have endured, Eastman addressed many of the issues which still confront Indians and which many of today's Native American authors continue to keep alive.

NOTES

1. See for example, *Nation* 103 (July–December 1916): 541–42; *North American Review* 204 (July–December 1916): 947–48; *Independent* 88 (October–December 1916): 464; *Literary Digest* 53 (July–December 1916): 1546; ALA *Booklist* 13 (1916–17): 115–16; *New York Times*, December 24, 1916.

2. Charles A. Eastman to H. M. Hitchcock, September 8, 1927, H. M. Hitchcock Papers, Ayer Collection, Newberry Library, Chicago, Illinois.

3. See Charles A. Eastman, *Indian Boyhood* (1902; reprint ed., Dover Publications, 1971), pp. 243–47.

4. Charles A. Eastman, *The Indian Today: The Past and Future of the First American* (Garden City, N.Y.: Doubleday, Page, & Co., 1915), pp. 43, 113–14; Charles A. Eastman, "The Indian's Plea for Freedom," *American Indian Magazine* 6 (Winter 1919): 164.

5. Eastman, "The Indian's Plea for Freedom," p. 165; U.S. Congress, House Subcommittee on Indian Affairs, *Peyote Hearings*, 1918, pt. I, pp. 139–41, 164.

6. Eastman to Hitchcock, September 21, 1930, Hitchcock Papers.

FOREWORD

"INDIAN BOYHOOD," published first in 1902 and in many subsequent editions, pictures the first of three distinct periods in the life of the writer of this book. His childhood and youth were a part of the free wilderness life of the first American—a life that is gone forever! By dint of much persuasion, the story has now been carried on from the point of that plunge into the unknown with which the first book ends, a change so abrupt and so overwhelming that the boy of fifteen "felt as if he were dead and travelling to the spirit land." We are now to hear of a single-hearted quest throughout eighteen years of adolescence and early maturity, for the attainment of the modern ideal of Christian culture: and again of a quarter of a century devoted to testing that hard-won standard in various fields of endeavor, partly by holding it up before his own race, and partly by interpreting their racial ideals to the white man, leading in the end to a partial reaction in favor of the earlier, the simpler, perhaps the more spiritual philosophy. It is clearly impossible to tell the whole story, but much that cannot be told may be read "between the lines." The broad outlines, the salient features of an uncommon experience are here set forth in the hope that they may strengthen for some readers the conception of our common humanity.

E.G.E.

CONTENTS

CHAPTER   PAGE

I THE WAY OPENS 1

II MY FIRST SCHOOL DAYS 14

III ON THE WHITE MAN'S TRAIL 31

IV COLLEGE LIFE IN THE WEST 51

V COLLEGE LIFE IN THE EAST 61

VI A DOCTOR AMONG THE INDIANS 76

VII THE GHOST DANCE WAR 92

VIII WAR WITH THE POLITICIANS 116

IX CIVILIZATION AS PREACHED AND PRAC-

   TISED 136

X AT THE NATION'S CAPITAL 151

XI BACK TO THE WOODS 166

XII THE SOUL OF THE WHITE MAN 182

LIST OF ILLUSTRATIONS

Charles A. Eastman (Ohiyesa). *Frontispiece*

FACING PAGE

Many Lightnings. English name, Jacob
Eastman. From an old daguerreotype
of Dr. Eastman's father 6
Typical Indian log cabin, such as Dr. East-
man's father lived in at Flandreau,
Dakota Territory 16
At home in the wilderness. A group of
Indian teepees 16
Santee Normal Training School, Santee,
Nebraska, as it looks to-day 32
Rev. Alfred L. Riggs, Superintendent Santee
Training School 40
Part of Class of '87, Dartmouth College,
after a "Rush." Eastman in centre,
front 66
Mrs. Frank Wood, of Boston; Eastman's
"White Mother" 72

xxi

List of Illustrations

FACING PAGE

Eastman at Knox College, 1880 76

Eastman in 1890, when he took his medical
    degree at Boston University 76

Chapel of the Holy Cross, Pine Ridge
    Agency, used as hospital for wounded
    Indians during the "Ghost Dance
    War" 80

Pine Ridge Agency, 1890 80

Mato-wa-nahtaka (Kicking Bear), High
    Priest of the "Messiah Craze," 1890–
    91 100

Elaine Goodale Eastman 126

Ohiyesa the Second, at five years of age,
    1903 152

With guide and bark canoe, on Rainy Lake,
    Ontario 176

FROM THE DEEP WOODS TO CIVILIZATION

I

THE WAY OPENS

ONE can never be sure of what a day may bring to pass. At the age of fifteen years, the deepening current of my life swung upon such a pivotal day, and in the twinkling of an eye its whole course was utterly changed; as if a little mountain brook should pause and turn upon itself to gather strength for the long journey toward an unknown ocean.

From childhood I was consciously trained to be a man; that was, after all, the basic thing; but after this I was trained to be a warrior and a hunter, and not to care for money or possessions, but to be in the broadest sense a public servant. After arriving

1

at a reverent sense of the pervading presence of the Spirit and Giver of Life, and a deep consciousness of the brotherhood of man, the first thing for me to accomplish was to adapt myself perfectly to natural things — in other words, to harmonize myself with nature. To this end I was made to build a body both symmetrical and enduring — a house for the soul to live in — a sturdy house, defying the elements. I must have faith and patience; I must learn self-control and be able to maintain silence. I must do with as little as possible and start with nothing most of the time, because a true Indian always shares whatever he may possess.

I felt no hatred for our tribal foes. I looked upon them more as the college athlete regards his rivals from another college. There was no thought of destroying a nation, taking away their country or reducing the people to servitude, for my race rather honored and bestowed gifts upon their enemies at the next peaceful meeting, until they had adopted the usages of the white man's warfare for spoliation and conquest.

There was one unfortunate thing about

my early training, however; that is, I was taught never to spare a citizen of the United States, although we were on friendly terms with the Canadian white men. The explanation is simple. My people had been turned out of some of the finest country in the world, now forming the great states of Minnesota and Iowa. The Americans pretended to buy the land at ten cents an acre, but never paid the price; the debt stands unpaid to this day. Because they did not pay, the Sioux protested; finally came the outbreak of 1862 in Minnesota, when many settlers were killed, and forthwith our people, such as were left alive, were driven by the troops into exile.

My father, who was among the fugitives in Canada, had been betrayed by a half-breed across the United States line, near what is now the city of Winnipeg. Some of the party were hanged at Fort Snelling, near St. Paul. We supposed, and, in fact, we were informed that all were hanged. This was why my uncle, in whose family I lived, had taught me never to spare a white man from the United States.

From the Deep Woods to Civilization

During the summer and winter of 1871, the band of Sioux to which I belonged — a clan of the Wah petons, or "Dwellers among the Leaves" — roamed in the upper Missouri region and along the Yellowstone River. In that year I tasted to the full the joy and plenty of wild existence. I saw buffalo, elk, and antelope in herds numbering thousands. The forests teemed with deer, and in the "Bad Lands" dwelt the Big Horns or Rocky Mountain sheep. At this period, grizzly bears were numerous and were brought into camp quite commonly, like any other game.

We frequently met and camped with the Hudson Bay half-breeds in their summer hunt of the buffalo, and we were on terms of friendship with the Assiniboines and the Crees, but in frequent collision with the Blackfeet, the Gros Ventres, and the Crows. However, there were times of truce when all met in peace for a great midsummer festival and exchange of gifts. The Sioux roamed over an area nearly a thousand miles in extent. In the summer we gathered together in large numbers, but towards fall

4

we would divide into small groups or bands
and scatter for the trapping and the winter
hunt. Most of us hugged the wooded river
bottoms; some depended entirely upon
the buffalo for food, while others, and among
these my immediate kindred, hunted all
kinds of game, and trapped and fished as
well.

Thus I was trained thoroughly for an all-
round out-door life and for all natural
emergencies. I was a good rider and a good
shot with the bow and arrow, alert and alive
to everything that came within my ken.
I had never known nor ever expected to
know any life but this.

In the winter and summer of 1872, we
drifted toward the southern part of what is
now Manitoba. In this wild, rolling country
I rapidly matured, and laid, as I supposed,
the foundations of my life career, never
dreaming of anything beyond this manful
and honest, unhampered existence. My
horse and my dog were my closest companions. I regarded them as brothers, and if
there was a hereafter, I expected to meet
them there. With them I went out daily

into the wilderness to seek inspiration and
store up strength for coming manhood.
My teachers dreamed no more than I of any
change in my prospects. I had now taken
part in all our tribal activities except that
of war, and was nearly old enough to be
initiated into the ritual of the war-path.
The world was full of natural rivalry; I
was eager for the day.

I had attained the age of fifteen years and
was about to enter into and realize a man's
life, as we Indians understood it, when the
change came. One fine September morning
as I returned from the daily hunt, there
seemed to be an unusual stir and excitement
as I approached our camp. My faithful
grandmother was on the watch and met me
to break the news. "Your father has come
— he whom we thought dead at the hands
of the white men," she said.

It was a day of miracle in the deep Canadian wilderness, before the Canadian Pacific
had been even dreamed of, while the Indian
and the buffalo still held sway over the vast
plains of Manitoba east of the Rocky Mountains. It was, perhaps, because he was my

MANY LIGHTNINGS. ENGLISH NAME, JACOB EASTMAN.
FROM AN OLD DAGUERREOTYPE OF
DR. EASTMAN'S FATHER.

honored father that I lent my bewildered ear
to his eloquent exposition of the so-called
civilized life, or the way of the white man.
I could not doubt my own father, so myste-
riously come back to us, as it were, from the
spirit land; yet there was a voice within
saying to me, "A false life! a treacherous
life!"

In accordance with my training, I asked
few questions, although many arose in my
mind. I simply tried silently to fit the new
ideas like so many blocks into the pattern of
my philosophy, while according to my un-
tutored logic some did not seem to have
straight sides or square corners to fit in with
the cardinal principles of eternal justice.
My father had been converted by Protestant
missionaries, and he gave me a totally new
vision of the white man, as a religious man
and a kindly. But when he related how
he had set apart every seventh day for religious duties and the worship of God, laying
aside every other occupation on that day, I
could not forbear exclaiming, "Father! and
does he then forget God during the six days
and do as he pleases?"

7

"Our own life, I will admit, is the best in a world of our own, such as we have enjoyed for ages," said my father. "But here is a race which has learned to weigh and measure everything, time and labor and the results of labor, and has learned to accumulate and preserve both wealth and the records of experience for future generations. You yourselves know and use some of the wonderful inventions of the white man, such as guns and gunpowder, knives and hatchets, garments of every description, and there are thousands of other things both beautiful and useful.

"Above all, they have their Great Teacher, whom they call Jesus, and he taught them to pass on their wisdom and knowledge to all other races. It is true that they have subdued and taught many peoples, and our own must eventually bow to this law; the sooner we accept their mode of life and follow their teaching, the better it will be for us all. I have thought much on this matter and such is my conclusion."

There was a mingling of admiration and indignation in my mind as I listened. My father's two brothers were still far from being

8

convinced; but filial duty and affection over-
weighed all my prejudices. I was bound
to go back with him as he desired me to do,
and my grandmother and her only daughter
accompanied us on the perilous journey.

The line between Canada and the United
States was closely watched at this time by
hostile Indians, therefore my father thought
it best to make a dash for Devil's Lake, in
North Dakota, where he could get assistance
if necessary. He knew Major Forbes, who
was in command of the military post and the
agency. Our guide we knew to be an un-
scrupulous man, who could easily betray us
for a kettle of whisky or a pony. One of the
first things I observed was my father's
reading aloud from a book every morning
and evening, followed by a very strange song
and a prayer. Although all he said was in
Indian, I did not understand it fully. He
apparently talked aloud to the "Great
Mystery", asking for our safe guidance back
to his home in the States. The first reading
of this book of which I have any recollection
was the twenty-third Psalm, and the first
hymn he sang in my presence was to the old

9

tune of Ortonville. It was his Christian
faith and devotion which was perhaps the
strongest influence toward my change of
heart and complete change of my purpose
in life.

I think it was at our second encampment
that we met a large caravan of Canadian
half-breeds accompanied by a band of Northern Ojibways. As was usual with the former,
they had plenty of whisky. They were
friendly enough with us, at least while sober,
but the Indians were not. Father showed
them his papers as a United States citizen
and a letter from Major Forbes, telling of his
peaceful mission, but we could not trust
our ancestral enemies, the Ojibways, especially when excited with strong drink. My
father was calm and diplomatic throughout,
but thus privately instructed me:

"My son, conceal yourself in the woods;
and if the worst comes you must flee on your
swift pony. Before daylight you can pass
the deep woods and cross the Assiniboine
River." He handed me a letter to Major
Forbes. I said, "I will try," and as soon as
it was dark, I hid myself, to be in readiness.

Meanwhile, my father called the leading half-breeds together and told them again that he was under the protection of his government, also that the Sioux would hold them responsible if anything happened to us. Just then they discovered that another young brave and I were not to be found, which made them think that father had dispatched us to the nearest military post for help. They immediately led away their drunken comrades and made a big talk to their Ojibway friends, so that we remained undisturbed until morning.

Some days later, at the south end of Devil's Lake, I left our camp early to shoot some ducks when the morning flight should begin. Suddenly, when out of sight of the others, my eye caught a slight movement in the rank grass. Instinctively I dropped and flattened myself upon the ground, but soon a quick glance behind me showed plainly the head of a brave hidden behind a bush. I waited, trying to figure out some plan of escape, yet facing the probability that I was already surrounded, until I caught sight of another head almost in front and still another to my left.

11

In the moments that elapsed after I fully realized my situation, I thought of almost everything that had happened to me up to that day; of a remarkable escape from the Ojibways, of the wild pets I had had, and of my playmates in the Canadian camps whom I should never see again. I also thought with more curiosity than fear of the "Great Mystery" that I was so soon to enter. As these thoughts were passing through my mind, I carelessly moved and showed myself plainly to the enemy.

Suddenly, from behind the nearest bush, came the sound of my own Sioux tongue and the words, "Are you a Sioux?" Possibly my countenance may not have changed much, but certainly I grew weak with surprise and relief. As soon as I answered "Yes!" I was surrounded by a group of warriors of my tribe, who chuckled at the joke that had come so near to costing me my life, for one of them explained that he had been on the point of firing when I exposed myself so plainly that he saw I was not an Ojibway in war paint but probably a Sioux like himself.

After a variety of adventures, we arrived

12

at the canvas city of Jamestown, then the terminal point of the Northern Pacific railroad. I was out watering the ponies when a terrific peal of thunder burst from a spotless blue sky, and indeed seemed to me to be running along the surface of the ground. The terrified ponies instantly stampeded, and I confess I was not far behind them, when a monster with one fiery eye poked his head around a corner of the hill. When we reached camp, my father kindly explained, and I was greatly relieved.

It was a peaceful Indian summer day when we reached Flandreau, in Dakota Territory, the citizen Indian settlement, and found the whole community gathered together to congratulate and welcome us home.

II

MY FIRST SCHOOL DAYS

IT was less than a month since I had been a
rover and a hunter in the Manitoba wilderness, with no thoughts save those which
concern the most free and natural life of an
Indian. Now, I found myself standing near
a rude log cabin on the edge of a narrow
strip of timber, overlooking the fertile basin
of the Big Sioux River. As I gazed over the
rolling prairie land, all I could see was that
it met the sky at the horizon line. It seemed
to me vast and vague and endless, as was my
conception of the new trail which I had taken
and my dream of the far-off goal.

My father's farm of 160 acres, which he had
taken up and improved under the United
States homestead laws, lay along the north
bank of the river. The nearest neighbor
lived a mile away, and all had flourishing
fields of wheat, Indian corn and potatoes.

My First School Days

Some two miles distant, where the Big Sioux doubled upon itself in a swinging loop, rose the mission church and schoolhouse, the only frame building within forty miles.

Our herd of ponies was loose upon the prairie, and it was my first task each morning to bring them into the log corral. On this particular morning I lingered, finding some of them, like myself, who loved their freedom too well and would not come in.

The man who had built the cabin — it was his first house, and therefore he was proud of it — was tall and manly looking. He stood in front of his pioneer home with a resolute face.

He had been accustomed to the buffalo-skin teepee all his life, until he opposed the white man and was defeated and made a prisoner of war at Davenport, Iowa. It was because of his meditations during those four years in a military prison that he had severed himself from his tribe and taken up a homestead. He declared that he would never join in another Indian outbreak, but would work with his hands for the rest of his life.

"I have hunted every day," he said, "for the support of my family. I sometimes chase

15

the deer all day. One must work, and work
hard, whether chasing the deer or planting
corn. After all, the corn-planting is the
surer provision."

These were my father's new views, and in
this radical change of life he had persuaded
a few other families to join him. They
formed a little colony at Flandreau, on the
Big Sioux River.

To be sure, his beginnings in civilization
had not been attended with all the success
that he had hoped for. One year the crops
had been devoured by grasshoppers, and
another year ruined by drought. But he was
still satisfied that there was no alternative
for the Indian. He was now anxious to have
his boys learn the English language and something about books, for he could see that
these were the "bow and arrows" of the
white man.

"O-hee-ye-sa!" called my father, and I
obeyed the call. "It is time for you to go to
school, my son," he said, with his usual air of
decision. We had spoken of the matter
more than once, yet it seemed hard when it
came to the actual undertaking.

Typical Indian Log Cabin, such as Dr. Eastman's Father
lived in at Flandreau, Dakota Territory.

At Home in the Wilderness. A Group of Indian Teepees.

My First School Days

I remember quite well how I felt as I stood there with eyes fixed upon the ground.

"And what am I to do at the school?" I asked finally, with much embarrassment.

"You will be taught the language of the white man, and also how to count your money and tell the prices of your horses and of your furs. The white teacher will first teach you the signs by which you can make out the words on their books. They call them A, B, C, and so forth. Old as I am, I have learned some of them."

The matter having been thus far explained, I was soon on my way to the little mission school, two miles distant over the prairie. There was no clear idea in my mind as to what I had to do, but as I galloped along the road I turned over and over what my father had said, and the more I thought of it the less I was satisfied. Finally I said aloud:

"Why do we need a sign language, when we can both hear and talk?" And unconsciously I pulled on the lariat and the pony came to a stop. I suppose I was half curious and half in dread about this "learning white men's ways." Meanwhile the pony had begun to graze.

While thus absorbed in thought, I was suddenly startled by the yells of two other Indian boys and the noise of their ponies' hoofs. I pulled the pony's head up just as the two strangers also pulled up and stopped their panting ponies at my side. They stared at me for a minute, while I looked at them out of the corners of my eyes.

"Where are you going? Are you going to our school?" volunteered one of the boys at last.

To this I replied timidly: "My father told me to go to a place where the white men's ways are taught, and to learn the sign language."

"That's good — we are going there too! Come on, Red Feather, let's try another race! I think, if we had not stopped, my pony would have outrun yours. Will you race with us?" he continued, addressing me; and we all started our ponies at full speed.

I soon saw that the two strange boys were riding erect and soldier-like. "That must be because they have been taught to be like the white man," I thought. I allowed my pony a free start and leaned forward until the animal drew deep breaths, then I slid back and laid my head against the pony's shoulder, at the same time raising my quirt, and he leaped forward with a will! I yelled as I passed the other boys, and pulled up when I reached the crossing. The others stopped, too, and surveyed pony and rider from head to foot, as if they had never seen us before.

"You have a fast pony. Did you bring him back with you from Canada?" Red Feather asked. "I think you are the son of Many Lightnings, whom he brought home the other day," the boy added.

"Yes, this is my own pony. My uncle in Canada always used him to chase the buffalo, and he has ridden him in many battles." I spoke with considerable pride.

"Well, as there are no more buffalo to chase now, your pony will have to pull the plow like the rest. But if you ride him to school, you can join in the races. On the holy days the young men race horses, too."

Red Feather and White Fish spoke both together, while I listened attentively, for everything was strange to me.

"What do you mean by the 'holy days'?" I asked.

"Well, that's another of the white people's customs. Every seventh day they call a 'holy day', and on that day they go to a 'Holy House', where they pray to their Great Mystery. They also say that no one should work on that day."

This definition of Sunday and church-going set me to thinking again, for I never knew before that there was any difference in the days.

"But how do you count the days, and how do you know what day to begin with?" I inquired.

"Oh, that's easy! The white men have everything in their books. They know how many days in a year, and they have even divided the day itself into so many equal parts; in fact, they have divided them again and again until they know how many times one can breathe in a day," said White Fish, with the air of a learned man.

"That's impossible," I thought, so I shook my head.

By this time we had reached the second crossing of the river, on whose bank stood the little mission school. Thirty or forty Indian children stood about, curiously watching the newcomer as we came up the steep bank. I realized for the first time that I was an object of curiosity, and it was not a pleasant feeling. On the other hand, I was considerably interested in the strange appearance of these school-children.

They all had on some apology for white man's clothing, but their pantaloons belonged neither to the order *short* nor to the *long*. Their coats, some of them, met only halfway by the help of long strings. Others were lapped over in front, and held on by a string of some sort fastened round the body. Some of their hats were brimless and others without crowns, while most were fantastically painted. The hair of all the boys was cut short, and, in spite of the evidences of great effort to keep it down, it stood erect like porcupine quills. I thought, as I stood on one side and took a careful observation of the

motley gathering, that if I had to look like
these boys in order to obtain something of the
white man's learning, it was time for me to
rebel.

The boys played ball and various other
games, but I tied my pony to a tree and then
walked up to the schoolhouse and stood
there as still as if I had been glued to the wall.
Presently the teacher came out and rang a
bell, and all the children went in, but I waited
for some time before entering, and then slid
inside and took the seat nearest the door.
I felt singularly out of place, and for the
twentieth time wished my father had not
sent me.

When the teacher spoke to me, I had not
the slightest idea what he meant, so I did not
trouble myself to make any demonstration,
for fear of giving offense. Finally he asked
in broken Sioux: "What is your name?"
Evidently he had not been among the Indians
long, or he would not have asked that question. It takes a tactician and a diplomat to
get an Indian to tell his name! The poor
man was compelled to give up the attempt
and resume his seat on the platform.

He then gave some unintelligible directions, and, to my great surprise, the pupils in turn held their books open and talked the talk of a strange people. Afterward the teacher made some curious signs upon a blackboard on the wall, and seemed to ask the children to read them. To me they did not compare in interest with my bird's-track and fish-fin studies on the sands. I was something like a wild cub caught overnight, and appearing in the corral next morning with the lambs. I had seen nothing thus far to prove to me the good of civilization.

Meanwhile the children grew more familiar, and whispered references were made to the "new boy's" personal appearance. At last he was called "Baby" by one of the big boys; but this was not meant for him to hear, so he did not care to hear. He rose silently and walked out. He did not dare to do or say anything in departing. The boys watched him as he led his pony to the river to drink and then jumped upon his back and started for home at a good pace. They cheered as he started over the hills: "Hoo-oo! hoo-oo! there goes the long-haired boy!"

When I was well out of sight of the school, I pulled in my pony and made him walk slowly home.

"Will going to that place make a man brave and strong?" I asked myself. "I must tell my father that I cannot stay here. I must go back to my uncle in Canada, who taught me to hunt and shoot and to be a brave man. They might as well try to make a buffalo build houses like a beaver as to teach me to be a white man," I thought.

It was growing late when at last I appeared at the cabin. "Why, what is the matter?" quoth my old grandmother, who had taken especial pride in me as a promising young hunter. Really, my face had assumed a look of distress and mental pressure that frightened the superstitious old woman. She held her peace, however, until my father returned.

"Ah," she said then, "I never fully believed in these new manners! The Great Mystery cannot make a mistake. I say it is against our religion to change the customs that have been practiced by our people ages back — so far back that no one can remember it. Many of the school-children have died, you have told me. It is not strange. You have offended Him, because you have made these children change the ways he has given us. I must know more about this matter before I give my consent." Grandmother had opened her mind in unmistakable terms, and the whole family was listening to her in silence.

Then my hard-headed father broke the pause. "Here is one Sioux who will sacrifice everything to win the wisdom of the white man! We have now entered upon this life, and there is no going back. Besides, one would be like a hobbled pony without learning to live like those among whom we must live."

During father's speech my eyes had been fixed upon the burning logs that stood on end in the huge mud chimney in a corner of the cabin. I didn't want to go to that place again; but father's logic was too strong for me, and the next morning I had my long hair cut, and started in to school in earnest.

I obeyed my father's wishes, and went regularly to the little day-school, but as yet my mind was in darkness. What has all this

talk of books to do with hunting, or even
with planting corn? I thought. The subject occupied my thoughts more and more,
doubtless owing to my father's decided position on the matter; while, on the other hand,
my grandmother's view of this new life was
not encouraging.

I took the situation seriously enough, and
I remember I went with it where all my people
go when they want light — into the thick
woods. I needed counsel, and human counsel
did not satisfy me. I had been taught to
seek the "Great Mystery" in silence, in the
deep forest or on the height of the mountain.
There were no mountains here, so I retired
into the woods. I knew nothing of the white
man's religion; I only followed the teaching
of my ancestors.

When I came back, my heart was strong.
I desired to follow the new trail to the end.
I knew that, like the little brook, it must lead
to larger and larger ones until it became a
resistless river, and I shivered to think of it.
But again I recalled the teachings of my
people, and determined to imitate their
undaunted bravery and stoic resignation.

However, I was far from having realized the long, tedious years of study and confinement before I could begin to achieve what I had planned.

"You must not fear to work with your hands," said my father, "but if you are able to think strongly and well, that will be a quiver full of arrows for you, my son. All of the white man's children must go to school, but those who study best and longest need not work with their hands after that, for they can work with their minds. You may plow the five acres next the river, and see if you can make a straight furrow as well as a straight shot."

I set to work with the heavy breaking-plow and yoke of oxen, but I am sorry to admit that the work was poorly done. "It will be better for you to go away to a higher school," advised my father.

It appears remarkable to me now that my father, thorough Indian as he was, should have had such deep and sound conceptions of a true civilization. But there is the contrast — my father's mother! whose faith in her people's philosophy and training could not be superseded by any other allegiance.

To her such a life as we lead to-day would be no less than sacrilege. "It is not a true life," she often said. "It is a sham. I cannot bear to see my boy live a made-up life!"

Ah, grandmother! you had forgotten one of the first principles of your own teaching, namely: "When you see a new trail, or a footprint that you do not know, follow it to the point of knowing."

"All I want to say to you," the old grandmother seems to answer, "is this: Do not get lost on this new trail."

"I find," said my father to me, "that the white man has a well-grounded religion, and teaches his children the same virtues that our people taught to theirs. The Great Mystery has shown to the red and white man alike the good and evil, from which to choose. I think the way of the white man is better than ours, because he is able to preserve on paper the things he does not want to forget. He records everything — the sayings of his wise men, the laws enacted by his counselors."

My First School Days

I began to be really interested in this curious scheme of living that my father was gradually unfolding to me out of his limited experience.

"The way of knowledge," he continued, "is like our old way in hunting. You begin with a mere trail — a footprint. If you follow that faithfully, it may lead you to a clearer trail — a track — a road. Later on there will be many tracks, crossing and diverging one from the other. Then you must be careful, for success lies in the choice of the right road. You must be doubly careful, for traps will be laid for you, of which the most dangerous is the spirit-water, that causes a man to forget his self-respect," he added, unwittingly giving to his aged mother material for her argument against civilization.

The general effect upon me of these discussions, which were logical enough on the whole, although almost entirely from the outside, was that I became convinced that my father was right.

My grandmother had to yield at last, and it was settled that I was to go to school at

Santee agency, Nebraska, where Dr. Alfred
L. Riggs was then fairly started in the work
of his great mission school, which has turned
out some of the best educated Sioux Indians.
It was at that time the Mecca of the Sioux
country; even though Sitting Bull and Crazy
Horse were still at large, harassing soldiers
and emigrants alike, and General Custer had
just been placed in military command of the
Dakota Territory.

III

ON THE WHITE MAN'S TRAIL

IT was in the fall of 1874 that I started
from Flandreau, then only an Indian
settlement, with a good neighbor of ours
on his way to Santee. There were only a
dozen houses or so at Sioux Falls, and the
whole country was practically uninhabited,
when we embarked in a home-made prairie
schooner, on that bright September morning.

I had still my Hudson Bay flintlock
gun, which I had brought down with me
from Canada the year before. I took that
old companion, with my shot-pouch and a
well-filled powder-horn. All I had besides
was a blanket, and an extra shirt. I wore
my hunting suit, which was a compromise
between Indian attire and a frontiersman's
outfit. I was about sixteen years old and
small of my age.

"Remember, my boy, it is the same as if

I sent you on your first war-path. I shall expect you to conquer," was my father's farewell. My good grandmother, who had brought me up as a motherless child, bestowed upon me her blessing. "Always remember," said she, "that the Great Mystery is good; evil can come only from ourselves!" Thus I parted with my first teacher — the woman who taught me to pray!

Our first night out was at Hole-in-the-Hill, one of the most picturesque spots in the valley. Here I brought in a doe, which I had come upon in the tall grass of the river bottom. Peter shot several ducks, and we had a good supper. It seemed to me more like one of our regular fall hunts than like going away to school.

After supper I said, "I am going to set some of your traps, uncle."

"And I will go with you," replied Peter. "But before we go, we must have our prayer," and he took out his Bible and hymn-book printed in the Indian tongue.

It was all odd enough to me, for although my father did the same, I had not yet become

Santee Normal Training School, Santee, Nebraska, as it looks today. No. 1 is the old Chapel; No. 2, the Dakota Home.

thoroughly used to such things. Nevertheless, it was the new era for the Indian; and
while we were still seated on the ground
around the central fire of the Sioux teepee,
and had just finished our repast of wild game,
Peter read from the good book, and performed the devotional exercises of his teepee
home, with quite as much zeal as if he were
within four walls and surrounded by civilized
things. I was very much impressed when
this primitive Christian prayed that I might
succeed in my new undertaking.

The next morning was frosty, and after
an early breakfast we hurried to our traps.
I got two fine minks and a beaver for my
trouble, while Peter came home smiling
with two otters and three beaver. I saw
that he had something on his mind, but,
like a true Indian, I held my peace. At
last he broke the news to me — he had
changed his mind about going to Santee
agency!

I did not blame him — it was hard to
leave such a trapper's paradise as this,
alive with signs of otter, mink, and beaver.
I said nothing, but thought swiftly. The

33

temptation was strong to remain and trap too. That would please my grandmother; and I will confess here that no lover is more keen to do the right thing for the loved one than I was at that time to please my old grandmother.

The thought of my father's wish kept me on my true course. Leaving my gun with Peter, I took my blanket on my back and started for the Missouri on foot.

"Tell my father," I said, "that I shall not return ˙until I finish my war-path."

But the voice of the waterfall, near what is now the city of Sioux Falls, sounded like the spirits of woods and water crying for their lost playmate, and I thought for a moment of turning back to Canada, there to regain my freedom and wild life. Still, I had sent word to my father that this war-path should be completed, and I remembered how he had said that if I did not return, he would shed proud tears.

About this time I did some of the hardest thinking that I have ever done in my life. All day I traveled, and did not see any one until, late in the afternoon, descending into

the valley of a stream, I came suddenly
upon a solitary farm-house of sod, and was
met by a white man — a man with much
hair on his face.

I was hungry and thirsty as a moose in
burned timber. I had some money that my
father had given me — I hardly knew the
different denominations; so I showed the
man all of it, and told him by signs that he
might take what he pleased if only he would
let me have something to eat, and a little
food to carry with me. As for lodging, I
would not have slept in his house if he had
promised me a war-bonnet!

While he was cordial — at any rate,
after I exhibited my money — there was
something about his manner that did not
put me at my ease, and my wild instincts
told me to keep an eye on him. But I was
not alone in this policy, for his flock of four
daughters and a son nearly put their necks
out of joint in following my modest, shy
movements.

When they invited me to sit down with
them at the table, I felt uncomfortable,
but hunger was stronger than my fears

35

and modesty. The climax came when I took my seat on a rickety stool between the big, hairy man and one of his well-grown daughters. I felt not unlike a young blue heron just leaving the nest to partake of his first meal on an unsafe, swinging branch. I was entirely uncertain of my perch.

All at once, without warning, the man struck the table with the butt of his knife with such force that I jumped and was within an ace of giving a war-whoop. In spite of their taking a firm hold of the home-made table to keep it steady, the dishes were quivering, and the young ladies no longer able to maintain their composure. Severe glances from mother and father soon brought us calm, when it appeared that the blow on the table was merely a signal for quiet before saying grace. I pulled myself in, much as a turtle would do, and possibly it should be credited to the stoicism of my race that I scarcely ever ate a heartier meal.

After supper I got up and held out to the farmer nearly all the money I had. I did not care whether he took it all or not. I was grateful for the food, and money had

no such hold on my mind as it has gained
since. To my astonishment, he simply
smiled, shook his head, and stroked his
shaggy beard.

I was invited to join the family in the
sod-house parlor, but owing to the severe
nerve-shocks that I had experienced at
the supper-table, I respectfully declined,
and betook myself to the bank of the stream
near by, where I sat down to meditate.
Presently there pealed forth a peculiar,
weird music, and the words of a strange song.
It was music from a melodeon, but I did not
then know what that was; and the tune was
"Nearer, my God, to Thee." Strange as
it sounded to me, I felt that there was
something soothing and gentle about the
music and the voices.

After a while curiosity led me back to
the sod house, and I saw for the first time
how the white woman pumps so much air
into a box that when she presses on the top
boards it howls convulsively. I forgot my
bashfulness so far as to listen openly and
enjoy the operation, wondering much how the
white man puts a pair of lungs into a box,

which is furnished with a whole set of black and white teeth, and when he sings to it, it appears to answer him.

Presently I walked over to a shed where the farmer seemed to be very busy with his son, earnestly hammering something with all their might in the midst of glowing fire and sparks. He had an old breaking-plow which he was putting into shape on his rude forge. With sleeves rolled up, face and hands blackened and streaming with sweat, I thought he looked not unlike a successful warrior just returned from the field of battle. His powerful muscles and the manly way in which he handled the iron impressed me tremendously. "I shall learn that profession if ever I reach the school and learn the white man's way," I thought.

I thanked the good man for his kind invitation to sleep within the sod walls with all his family, but signed to him that I preferred to sleep out-of-doors. I could see some distrust in his eyes, for his horses were in the open stable; and at that my temper rose, but I managed to control it. He had been kind to me, and no Indian will break

38

the law of hospitality unless he has lost all
the trails of his people. The man looked
me over again carefully, and appeared
satisfied; and I rolled myself up in my
blanket among the willows, but every star
that night seemed to be bent upon telling
the story of the white man.

I slept little, and early the next morning
I was awakened by the barking of the
farmer's collie and the laughter of his
daughters. I got up and came to the house.
Breakfast was nearly ready, and every
member of the family was on hand. After
breakfast I once more offered my money,
but was refused. I was glad. Then and
there I loved civilization and renounced my
wild life.

I took up my blanket and continued on
my journey, which for three days was a
lonely one. I had nothing with which to
kill any game, so I stopped now and then
at a sod house for food. When I reached
the back hills of the Missouri, there lay
before me a long slope leading to the river
bottom, and upon the broad flat, as far as
my eyes could reach, lay farm-houses and

39

farms. Ah! I thought, this is the way of civilization, the basis upon which it rests! I desired to know that life.

Thirty miles from the school I met Dr. Riggs on the road, coming to the town of Yankton, and received some encouraging words from him, for he spoke the Sioux language very well. A little further on I met the Indian agent, Major Sears, a Quaker, and he, too, gave me a word of encouragement when he learned that I had walked a hundred and fifty miles to school. My older brother John, who was then assistant teacher and studying under Dr. Riggs, met me at the school and introduced me to my new life.

The bell of the old chapel at Santee summoned the pupils to class. Our principal read aloud from a large book and offered prayer. Although he conducted devotional exercises in the Sioux language, the subject matter was still strange, and the names he used were unintelligible to me. "Jesus" and "Jehovah" fell upon my ears as mere meaningless sounds.

I understood that he was praying to the "Great Mystery" that the work of the day

40

REV. ALFRED L. RIGGS, SUPERINTENDENT SANTEE
TRAINING SCHOOL.

might be blessed and their labor be fruitful. A cold sweat came out upon me as I heard him ask the "Great Mystery" to be with us in that day's work in that school building. I thought it was too much to ask of Him. I had been taught that the Supreme Being is only concerned with spirits, and that when one wishes to commune with Him in nature he must be in a spiritual attitude, and must retire from human sound or influence, alone in the wilderness. Here for the first time I heard Him addressed openly in the presence of a house full of young men and young girls!

All the scholars were ordered to various rooms under different instructors, and I was left in the chapel with another long-haired young man. He was a Mandan from Fort Berthold — one of our ancient enemies. Not more than two years before that time my uncle had been on the war-path against this tribe and had brought home two Mandan scalps. He, too, was a new scholar, and looked as if he were about to come before the judge to receive his sentence. My heart at once went out to him, although the

41

other pupils were all of my own tribe, the Sioux. I noticed that he had beautiful long hair arranged in two plaits, and in spite of his sad face he was noble-looking and appeared to great advantage, I thought, in contrast with the other pupils, whose hair was cut short and their garments not becoming to them at all. This boy, Alfred Mandan, became a very good friend of mine.

Dr. Riggs took me in hand and told me the rules of the school and what was expected of us. There was the chapel, which was used as a church every Sunday and as a schoolhouse on week days. There was the Dakota Home for the girls' dormitory — a small, square frame building — and for the boys a long log house some two hundred yards from the chapel under the large cotton-wood-trees.

Dr. Riggs said that I need not study that first day, but could fill up the big bag he brought me with straw from the straw pile back of his barn. I carried it over to the log cabin, where the Doctor was before me and had provided a bunk or framework for my bed. I filled a smaller bag for a pillow, and, having received the sheets and blankets, I made my first white man's bed under his supervision. When it was done it looked clean and dignified enough for any one, I thought.

He said that I must make it every morning like that before going to school. "And for your wash, there is a tin basin or two on a bench just outside of the door, by the water-barrels." And so it was. We had three barrels of Missouri River water, which we ourselves filled up every week, for we boys had to furnish our own water and wood, and were detailed in pairs for this work.

Dr. Riggs supplied axes for the wood-choppers, and barrels and pails for the water-carriers, also a yoke of large and gentle white oxen and a lumber-wagon. It seems to me that I never was better acquainted with two animals than with these two! I have done some of my solemnest thinking behind them. The Missouri River was about two miles from our log house, with a wide stretch of bottom land intervening, partly cottonwood timber and partly open meadow with tall grass. I could take a nap, or dance a war-dance, if I cared to do so, while they were carrying me to wood or to water.

Dr. Riggs gave me a little English primer to study, also one or two books in the Dakota language, which I had learned to read in the day-school. There was a translation of the Psalms, and of the Pilgrim's Progress. I must confess that at that time I would have preferred one of grandmother's evening stories, or my uncle's account of his day's experiences in the chase. I thought it was the dullest hunting I had ever known!

Toward evening a company of three young men arrived from up the river — to all appearance full-fledged warriors. Ah, it was good to see the handsome white, blue, and red blankets worn by these stately Sioux youths! I had not worn one since my return from Canada. My brother got me a suit of clothes, and had some one cut my hair, which was already over my ears, as it had not been touched since the year before. I felt like a wild goose with its wings clipped.

44

Next morning the day pupils emerged in every direction from the woods and deep ravines where the Indians had made their temporary homes, while we, the log-cabin boarders, came out in Indian file. The chapel bell was tolling as we reached the yard, when my attention was attracted to a pretty lass standing with her parents and Dr. Riggs near the Dakota Home. Then they separated and the father and mother came toward us, leaving the Doctor and the pretty Dakota maiden standing still. All at once the girl began to run toward her parents, screaming pitifully.

"Oh, I cannot, I cannot stay in the white man's house! I'll die, I'll die! Mamma! Mamma!"

The parents stopped and reasoned with the girl, but it was of no use. Then I saw them leading her back to the Dakota Home, in spite of her pleading and begging. The scene made my blood boil, and I suppressed with difficulty a strong desire to go to her aid.

How well I remember the first time we were called upon to recite! In the same

45

primer class were Eagle-Crane, Kite, and
their compatriot from up the river. For a
whole week we youthful warriors were held
up and harassed with words of three letters.
Like raspberry bushes in the path, they tore,
bled, and sweated us — those little words
rat, cat, and so forth — until not a semblance
of our native dignity and self-respect was
left. And we were of just the age when the
Indian youth is most on his dignity! Imagine the same fellows turned loose against
Custer or Harney with anything like equal
numbers and weapons, and those tried
generals would feel like boys! We had
been bred and trained to those things; but
when we found ourselves within four walls
and set to pick out words of three letters
we were like novices upon snow-shoes —
often flat on the ground.

I hardly think I was ever tired in my life
until those first days of boarding-school.
All day things seemed to come and pass
with a wearisome regularity, like walking
railway ties — the step was too short for
me. At times I felt something of the fascina-
tion of the new life, and again there would

arise in me a dogged resistance, and a voice seemed to be saying, "It is cowardly to depart from the old things!"

Aside from repeating and spelling words, we had to count and add imaginary amounts. We never had had any money to count, nor potatoes, nor turnips, nor bricks. Why, we valued nothing except honor; that cannot be purchased! It seemed now that everything must be measured in time or money or distance. And when the teacher placed before us a painted globe, and said that our world was like that — that upon such a thing our forefathers had roamed and hunted for untold ages, as it whirled and danced around the sun in space — I felt that my foothold was deserting me. All my savage training and philosophy was in the air, if these things were true.

Later on, when Dr. Riggs explained to us the industries of the white man, his thrift and forethought, we could see the reasonableness of it all. Economy is the able assistant of labor, and the two together produce great results. The systems and methods of business were of great interest to us, and especially the adoption of a medium of exchange.

The Doctor's own personality impressed us deeply, and his words of counsel and daily prayers, strange to us at first, in time found root in our minds. Next to my own father, this man did more than perhaps any other to make it possible for me to grasp the principles of true civilization. He also strengthened and developed in me that native strong ambition to win out, by sticking to whatever I might undertake. Associated with him was another man who influenced me powerfully toward Christian living. This was the Rev. Dr. John P. Williamson, the pioneer Presbyterian missionary. The world seemed gradually to unfold before me, and the desire to know all that the white man knows was the tremendous and prevailing thought in me, and was constantly growing upon me more and more.

My father wrote to me in the Dakota language for my encouragement. Dr. Riggs had told him that I was not afraid of books or of work, but rather determined to profit

48

by them. "My son," he wrote, "I believe that an Indian can learn all that is in the books of the white man, so that he may be equal to them in the ways of the mind!"

I studied harder than most of the boys. Missionaries were poor, and the Government policy of education for the Indian had not then been developed. The white man in general had no use for the Indian. Sitting Bull and the Northern Cheyennes were still fighting in Wyoming and Montana, so that the outlook was not bright for me to pursue my studies among the whites, yet it was now my secret dream and ambition.

It was at Santee that I sawed my first cord of wood. Before long I had a little money of my own, for I sawed most of Dr. Riggs's own wood and some at the Dakota Home, besides other work for which I was paid. Although I could not understand or speak much English, at the end of my second year I could translate every word of my English studies into the native tongue, besides having read all that was then published in the Sioux. I had caught up with

49

boys who had two or three years the start of me, and was now studying elementary algebra and geometry.

One day Dr. Riggs came to me and said that he had a way by which he could send me to Beloit, Wisconsin, to enter the preparatory department of Beloit College. This was a great opportunity, and I grasped it eagerly, though I had not yet lost my old timidity about venturing alone among the white people.

On the eve of departure, I received word from Flandreau that my father was dead, after only two days' illness. He was still in the prime of life and a tireless worker. This was a severe shock to me, but I felt even more strongly that I must carry out his wishes. It was clear that he who had sought me out among the wild tribes at the risk of his life, and set my feet in the new trail, should be obeyed to the end. I did not go back to my home, but in September, 1876, I started from Santee to Beloit to begin my serious studies.

IV

COLLEGE LIFE IN THE WEST

THE journey to Beloit College was an education in itself. At Yankton City I boarded the train for the first time in my life, but not before having made a careful inspection of the locomotive — that fiery monster which had so startled me on my way home from Canada. Every hour brought new discoveries and new thoughts — visions that came and passed like the telegraph poles as we sped by. More and more we seemed to me to be moving upon regions too small for the inhabitants. Towns and villages grew ever larger and nearer together, until at last we reached a city of some little size where it was necessary for me to change cars, a matter that had been arranged by Dr. Riggs with the conductor. The streets looked crowded and everybody seemed to be in the greatest possible hurry. I was

struck with the splendor of the shops and
the brilliant show windows. Some one took
me to an eating house and left me alone with
the pretty waitress, whose bright eyes and
fluent speech alarmed me. I thought it
best to agree with everything she said, so I
assented with a nod of the head, and I
fancy she brought me everything that was
on the bill of fare!

When I reached Beloit on the second day
of my pilgrimage, I found it beautifully
located on the high, wooded banks of Black
Hawk's picturesque Rock River. The college grounds covered the site of an ancient
village of mound-builders, which showed to
great advantage on the neat campus, where
the green grass was evenly cut with lawn-
mowers. I was taken to President Chapin's
house, and after a kindly greeting, shown
to my room in South College, where I immediately opened all the windows. A
young man emerged from our building
and I could distinctly hear him shouting
to another across the Common:

"Hurry up, Turkey, or you'll not have
the chance to face old Petty again! We

have Sitting Bull's nephew right here, and it's more than likely he'll have your scalplock before morning!"

"Turkey," as I soon learned, was the son of a missionary to that country, and both of these boys became good friends of mine afterward.

It must be remembered that this was September, 1876, less than three months after Custer's gallant command was annihilated by the hostile Sioux. I was especially troubled when I learned that my two uncles whom we left in Canada had taken part in this famous fight. People were bitter against the Sioux in those days, and I think it was a local paper that printed the story that I was a nephew of Sitting Bull, who had sent me there to study the white man's arts so that he might be better able to cope with him. When I went into the town, I was followed on the streets by gangs of little white savages, giving imitation war whoops.

My first recitation at Beloit was an event in my life. I was brought before a remarkable looking man whose name was Professor Pettibone. He had a long, grave face, with

long whiskers and scarcely any hair on his head, and was to me the very embodiment of wisdom. I was already well drilled in the elementary studies, except that I was very diffident about speaking the English language, and found it hard to recite or to demonstrate mathematical problems. However, I made every effort and soon learned to speak quite fluently, although not correctly; but that fact did not discourage me.

I was now a stranger in a strange country, and deep in a strange life from which I could not retreat. I was like a deaf man with eyes continually on the alert for the expression of faces, and to find them in general friendly toward me was somewhat reassuring. In spite of some nerve-trying moments, I soon recovered my balance and set to work. I absorbed knowledge through every pore. The more I got, the larger my capacity grew, and my appetite increased in proportion. I discovered that my anticipations of this new life were nearly all wrong, and was suddenly confronted with problems entirely foreign to my experience. If I had been told to swim across a lake, or run with a message

through an unknown country, I should have
had some conception of the task; but the
idea of each word as having an office and a
place and a specific name, and standing in
relation to other words like the bricks in
a wall, was almost beyond my grasp. As
for history and geography, to me they were
legends and traditions, and I soon learned
to appreciate the pure logic of mathematics.
A recent letter from a Beloit schoolmate
says, "You were the only boy who could
beat me in algebra!"

At Beloit I spent three years of student
life. While in some kinds of knowledge I
was the infant of the college, in athletics
I did my full share. To keep myself at my
best physically, I spent no less than three
hours daily in physical exercise, and this habit
was kept up throughout my college days.

I found among the students many who were
self-supporting, either the sons of poor
parents, or self-reliant youth who preferred
to earn money for at least a part of their
expenses. I soon discovered that these
young men were usually among the best
students. Since I had no means of my own,

and the United States Government had not then formulated the policy of Indian education, I was ready for any kind of work, and on Saturdays I usually sawed wood and did other chores for the professors.

During the first summer vacation I determined to hire out to a farmer. Armed with a letter of introduction from President Chapin, I set out in a southerly direction. As I walked, I recalled the troubles of that great chief of the Sac and Fox tribe, Black Hawk, who had some dispute with President Lincoln about that very region.

At the first farm I came to, I approached the front door with some misgivings. A young lady asked me to wait, and I fancied I read in her clear blue eyes the thoughts that passed through her mind. In ten minutes or so, the farmer came in from the field and entered his home by another door, apparently taking some precautions against a surprise before coming to me where I waited, hungry and tired, on the doorstep.

"Well, young man, what do you want?" quoth he.

I said, "I am a student of Beloit College,

but the college is closed for the summer and I am looking for work."

"Oho! you can not work the New Ulm game on me. I don't think you can reproduce the Fort Dearborn massacre on this farm. By the way, what tribe do you belong to?"

"I am Sioux," I replied.

"That settles it. Get off from my farm just as quick as you can! I had a cousin killed by your people only last summer."

I kept on my way until I found another farmer to whom I made haste to present my letter. For him I worked all summer, and as treaties were kept on both sides, there was no occasion for any trouble.

It was here and now that my eyes were opened intelligently to the greatness of Christian civilization, the ideal civilization, as it unfolded itself before my eyes. I saw it as the development of every natural resource; the broad brotherhood of mankind; the blending of all languages and the gathering of all races under one religious faith. There must be no more warfare within our borders; we must quit the forest trail for the breaking-plow, since pastoral life was the next thing for the Indian. I renounced finally my bow and arrows for the spade and the pen; I took off my soft moccasins and put on the heavy and clumsy but durable shoes. Every day of my life I put into use every English word that I knew, and for the first time permitted myself to think and act as a white man.

At the end of three years, other Sioux Indians had been sent to Beloit, and I felt that I might progress faster where I was not surrounded by my tribesmen. Dr. Riggs arranged to transfer me to the preparatory department of Knox College, at Galesburg, Ill., of which he was himself a graduate. Here, again, I was thrown into close contact with the rugged, ambitious sons of western farmers. Among my stanch friends at Knox were S. S. McClure, John S. Phillips of the *American Magazine*, Edgar A. Bancroft of Chicago, now attorney for the International Harvester Company, Judge Merritt Pinckney of Chicago, Representative Rainey, and other men who have become well known and whose friendship is still retained.

College Life in the West

As Knox is a co-educational institution, it was here that I mingled for the first time with the pale-face maidens, and as soon as I could shake off my Indian shyness, I found them very winning and companionable. It was through social intercourse with the American college girl that I gained my first conception of the home life and domestic ideals of the white man. I had thoroughly learned the Indian club and dumb bell exercises at Beloit, and here at Knox I was enabled by teaching them to a class of young ladies to meet a part of my expenses.

Soon I began to lay definite plans for the future. Happily, I had missed the demoralizing influences of reservation life, and had been mainly thrown with the best class of Christian white people. With all the strength of a clean young manhood, I set my heart upon the completion of a liberal education.

The next question to decide was what should be my special work in life. It appeared that in civilization one must have a definite occupation — a profession. I wished to share with my people whatever I might attain, and I looked about me for a distinct field of usefulness apart from the ministry, which was the first to be adopted by the educated Sioux.

Gradually my choice narrowed down to law and medicine, for both of which I had a strong taste; but the latter seemed to me to offer a better opportunity of service to my race; therefore I determined upon the study of medicine long before I entered upon college studies. "Hitch your wagon to a star," says the American philosopher, and this was my star!

V

COLLEGE LIFE IN THE EAST

ONE summer vacation, at my home in Dakota, Dr. Riggs told me the story of Dartmouth College in New Hampshire, and how it was originally founded as a school for Indian youth. The news was timely and good news; and yet I hesitated. I dreaded to cut myself off from my people, and in my heart I knew that if I went, I should not return until I had accomplished my purpose. It was a critical moment in my life, but the decision could be only one way. I taught the little day-school where my first lessons had been learned, throughout the fall term, and in January, 1882, I set out for the far East, at a period when the Government was still at considerable trouble to subdue and settle some of my race upon reservations.

Though a man in years, I had very little practical knowledge of the world, and in my inexperience I was still susceptible to the adventurous and curious side of things rather than to their profounder meanings. Therefore, while somewhat prepared, I was not yet conscious of the seriousness and terrific power of modern civilization.

It was a crisp winter morning when the train pulled into Chicago. I had in mind the Fort Dearborn incident, and it seemed to me that we were being drawn into the deep gulches of the Bad Lands as we entered the city. I realized vividly at that moment that the day of the Indian had passed forever.

I was met at the station by friends, who took me to walk upon some of the main streets. I saw a perfect stream of humanity rushing madly along, and noticed with some surprise that the faces of the people were not happy at all. They wore an intensely serious look that to me was appalling.

I was cautioned against trusting strangers, and told that I must look out for pickpockets. Evidently there were some disadvantages connected with this mighty civilization, for we Indians seldom found it necessary to guard our possessions. It seemed to me that the most dignified men on the streets were the policemen, in their long blue coats with brass buttons. They were such a remarkable set of men physically that this of itself was enough to catch my eye.

Soon I was again upon the eastern bound express, and we had not gone far when a middle-aged man who had thoroughly investigated my appearance both through and over his glasses, came to my seat and without apology or introduction began to bombard me with countless questions.

"You are an Indian?" he began.

"Yes," I murmured.

"What is your tribe?"

"Sioux."

"How came you so far away from the tribe? Are you a member of Sitting Bull's band? Are you related to him?" he continued. I was greatly relieved when he released me from his intrusive scrutiny. Among our people, the children and old women sometimes betray curiosity as regards a stranger, but no grown man would be guilty of such bad manners as I have often met with when traveling.

From the Deep Woods to Civilization

After we left Albany, I found myself in a
country the like of which, I thought, I
would have given much to hunt over before
it was stripped of its primeval forests, and
while deer and bears roamed over it undisturbed. I looked with delight upon
mountains and valleys, and even the little
hamlets perched upon the shelves of the
high hills. The sight of these rocky farms
and little villages reminded me of the presence of an earnest and persistent people.
Even the deserted farmhouse, the ruined
mill, had an air of saying, "I have done my
part in the progress of civilization. Now I
can rest." And all the mountains seemed
to say, Amen.

What is the great difference between these
people and my own? I asked myself. Is it
not that the one keeps the old things and
continually adds to them new improvements,
while the other is too well contented with
the old, and will not change his ways nor
seek to improve them?

When I reached Boston, I was struck with
the old, mossy, granite edifices, and the
narrow, crooked streets. Here, too, the

people hurried along as if the gray wolf were on their trail. Their ways impressed me as cold, but I forgot that when I had learned to know some of them better.

I went on to Dartmouth College, away up among the granite hills. The country around it is rugged and wild; and thinking of the time when red men lived here in plenty and freedom, it seemed as if I had been destined to come view their graves and bones. No, I said to myself, I have come to continue that which in their last struggle they proposed to take up, in order to save themselves from extinction; but alas! it was too late. Had our New England tribes but followed the example of that great Indian, Samson Occum, and kept up with the development of Dartmouth College, they would have brought forth leaders and men of culture. This was my ambition — that the Sioux should accept civilization before it was too late! I wished that our young men might at once take up the white man's way, and prepare themselves to hold office and wield influence in their native states. Although this hope has not been fully realized, I have the satisfaction of knowing that not a few Indians now hold positions of trust and exercise some political power.

At Dartmouth College I found the buildings much older and more imposing than any I had seen before. There was a true scholastic air about them; in fact, the whole village impressed me as touched with the spirit of learning and refinement. My understanding of English was now so much enlarged as to enable me to grasp current events, as well as the principles of civilization, in a more intelligent manner.

At Kimball Union Academy, the little ancient institution at which I completed my preparation for college by direction of President Bartlett of Dartmouth, I absorbed much knowledge of the New Englander and his peculiarities. I found Yankees of the uneducated class very Indian-like in their views and habits; a people of strong character, plain-spoken, and opinionated. However, I observed that the students of the academy and their parents were very frugal and saving. Nothing could have been more instructive to me, as we Indians are inclined

PART OF CLASS OF '87, DARTMOUTH COLLEGE, AFTER A "RUSH." EASTMAN IN CENTRE, FRONT.

to be improvident. I had been accustomed to broad, fertile prairies, and liberal ways. Here they seemed to count their barrels of potatoes and apples before they were grown. Every little brooklet was forced to do a river's work in their mills and factories.

I was graduated here and went to old Dartmouth in the fall of 1883 to enter the Freshman class. Although I had associated with college students for several years, yet I must confess that western college life is quiet compared with that of the tumultuous East. It was here that I had most of my savage gentleness and native refinement knocked out of me. I do not complain, for I know that I gained more than their equivalent.

On the evening of our first class meeting, lo! I was appointed football captain for my class. My supporters orated quite effectively on my qualifications as a frontier warrior, and some went so far as to predict that I would, when warmed up, scare all the Sophs off the premises! These representations seemed to be confirmed when, that same evening after supper, the two classes met in a first "rush," and as I was not acquainted with the men, I held up the professor of philosophy, mistaking him for one of the sophomores. Reporters for the Boston dailies made the most of their opportunity to enlarge upon this incident.

I was a sort of prodigal son of old Dartmouth, and nothing could have exceeded the heartiness of my welcome. The New England Indians, for whom it was founded, had departed well-nigh a century earlier, and now a warlike Sioux, like a wild fox, had found his way into this splendid seat of learning! Though poor, I was really better off than many of the students, since the old college took care of me under its ancient charter. I was treated with the greatest kindness by the president and faculty, and often encouraged to ask questions and express my own ideas. My uncle's observations in natural history, for which he had a positive genius, the Indian standpoint in sociology and political economy, these were the subject of some protracted discussions in the class room. This became so well understood, that some of my classmates who had failed to prepare their recitations would induce me to take up the time by advancing a native theory or first hand observation.

For the first time, I became really interested in literature and history. Here it was that civilization began to loom up before me colossal in its greatness, when the fact dawned upon me that nations and tongues, as well as individuals, have lived and died. There were two men of the past who were much in my thoughts: my countryman Occum, who matriculated there a century before me, and the great Daniel Webster (said to have a strain of Indian blood), who came to Dartmouth as impecunious as I was. It was under the Old Pine Tree that the Indians were supposed to have met for the last time to smoke the pipe of peace, and under its shadow every graduating class of my day smoked a parting pipe.

I was anxious to help myself as much as possible and gain practical experience at the same time, by working during the long summer vacations. One summer I worked in a hotel, at another time I canvassed for a book, I think it was the "Knights of Labor,"

69

published in Boston. Such success as I
attained was due less to any business sagac-
ity than to a certain curiosity I seemed to
excite, and which often resulted in the purchase of the book, whether the subscriber
really cared for it or not. Another summer,
an old school friend, an Armenian, con-
ceived the scheme of dressing me in native
costume and sending me out to sell his goods.
When I wore a jacket and fez, and was well
scented with attar of rose, no dog would
permit me on his master's premises if he
could help it; nevertheless I did very well.
For business purposes I was a Turk, but I
never answered any direct questions on the
subject of my nativity.

Throughout my student days in the West,
I had learned to reverence New England,
and especially its metropolis, as the home of
culture and art, of morality and Christianity.
At that period that sort of thing got a lodging
place in my savage mind more readily than
the idea of wealth or material power. Somehow I had supposed that Boston must be
the home of the nation's elect and not far
from the millenium. I was very happy

when, after my graduation with the class of
1887, it was made possible for me to study
medicine at Boston University. The friends
who generously assisted me to realize my
great ambition were of the type I had
dreamed of, and my home influences in
their family all that I could have wished for.
A high ideal of duty was placed before me,
and I was doubly armed in my original purpose to make my education of service to my
race. I continued to study the Christ
philosophy and loved it for its essential
truths, though doctrines and dogmas often
puzzled and repelled me. I attended the
Shawmut Congregational church, of which
the Rev. William Eliot Griffis was then
pastor, and I am happy to say he became my
life-long friend.

Mr. and Mrs. Frank Wood, who were a
father and mother to me at this period of
my life, were very considerate of my health
and gave me opportunity to enter into many
outdoor sports, such as tennis and canoeing,
beside regular gymnasium work. The unique
features of old Boston, the park system with
the public flower gardens and the Arboretum,

the reservoirs, and above all, the harbor with its vast assemblage of vessels, each of these was a school in itself. I did much general reading, and did not neglect my social opportunities. At Dartmouth I had met the English man of letters, Matthew Arnold, and he was kind enough to talk with me for some time. I have also talked with Emerson, Longfellow, Francis Parkman, and many other men of note. Mr. and Mrs. Wood were trustees of Wellesley College and I was so fortunate as to be an occasional visitor there, and to make the acquaintance of Miss Freeman, its first president. I believe the first lecture I ever delivered in public was before the Wellesley girls. I little dreamed that a daughter of mine would ever be among them! At another time I was asked by Mrs. Hemenway to give one of a course of eight historical lectures to the high school boys and girls. My subject was the French and Indian wars, especially the conspiracy of Pontiac. I had studied this period minutely and spoke for an hour and a quarter without any manuscript.

At the seaside hotels, I met society people

MRS. FRANK WOOD, OF BOSTON. EASTMAN'S " WHITE MOTHER."

of an entirely different sort to those I had
hitherto taken as American types. I was,
I admit, particularly struck with the audac-
ity and forwardness of the women. Among
our people the man always leads. I was
astonished to learn that some women whom
I had observed to accept the most marked
attentions from the men were married
ladies. Perhaps my earlier training had
been too Puritanical, or my æsthetic sense
was not then fully developed, for I was
surprised when I entered the ballroom to see
the pretty women clad so scantily.

One summer at Nantasket beach, I recall
that I had somehow been noted by an enter-
prising representative of a Boston daily,
who printed a column or so on my doings,
which were innocent enough. He good-
naturedly remarked that "the hero of the
Boston society girls just now is a Sioux
brave", etc. and described all the little
gifts of sofa cushions, pictures, and so on,
that I had ever received from my girl friends,
as well as the medals won in college. I never
knew who had let him into my room!

During the three years that I studied in

Boston, I went every summer to Mr. Moody's famous summer school at Northfield, and was much interested in his strong personality. One morning as we walked together, we came to a stone at the roadside. "Eastman," said he, "this stone is a reminder of the cruelty of your countrymen two centuries ago. Here they murdered an innocent Christian."

"Mr. Moody," I replied, "it might have been better if they had killed them all. Then you would not have had to work so hard to save the souls of their descendants."

At the date of my graduation, in 1890, the Government had fully committed itself to the new and permanent plan of educating the young Indians preparatory to admitting them to citizenship. Various philanthropic societies had been formed expressly to help toward this end. These facts gave weight and momentum to my desire to use all that I had learned for their benefit. I soon received my appointment to the position of Government physician at Pine Ridge agency in South Dakota, to report October first. Meantime I stayed in Boston and kept books for Mr. Wood while his bookkeeper took a vacation, and later secured an extension of time in order to attend the Lake Mohonk Indian conference. Here I met Mr. Herbert Welsh and Professor Painter of the Indian Rights association, Bishop Hare, Bishop Whipple, and many others, and listened with great interest to their discussions. I became convinced that the Indians had some real friends and this gave me much encouragement.

VI

A DOCTOR AMONG THE INDIANS

THE Pine Ridge Indian agency was a
bleak and desolate looking place in
those days, more especially in a November
dust storm such as that in which I arrived
from Boston to take charge of the medical
work of the reservation. In 1890 a "white
doctor" who was also an Indian was something of a novelty, and I was afterward informed that there were many and diverse
speculations abroad as to my success or
failure in this new rôle, but at the time I
was unconscious of an audience. I was
thirty-two years of age, but appeared much
younger, athletic and vigorous, and alive
with energy and enthusiasm.

After reporting to the Indian agent, I
was shown to my quarters, which consisted
of a bedroom, sitting room, office, and dispensary, all in one continuous barrack with the

EASTMAN AT KNOX COLLEGE, 1880.

EASTMAN IN 1890, WHEN HE TOOK HIS
MEDICAL DEGREE AT BOSTON
UNIVERSITY.

police quarters and the agent's offices. This barrack was a flimsy one-story affair built of warped cottonwood lumber, and the rude prairie winds whistled musically through the cracks. There was no carpet, no furniture save a plain desk and a couple of hard wooden chairs, and everything was coated with a quarter of an inch or so of fine Dakota dust. This did not disconcert me, however, as I myself was originally Dakota dust! An old-fashioned box stove was the only cheerful thing on the premises, and the first duty I performed was to myself. I built a roaring fire in the stove, and sat down for a few minutes to take a sort of inventory of the situation and my professional prospects.

I had not yet thought seriously of making a life contract with any young woman, and accordingly my place was at the agency mess where the unmarried employees took their meals. I recall that the cook at that time was a German, and the insistent sauerkraut and other German dishes were new to me and not especially appetizing.

After supper, as I sat alone in my dismal quarters fighting the first pangs of homesickness, an Indian softly opened the door and stepped in without knocking, in characteristic Indian fashion. My first caller was old Blue Horse, chief emeritus of the Loafer band, of which American Horse was the active chief. After greeting me in Sioux, he promptly produced his credentials, which consisted of well-worn papers that had been given him by various high military officers, from General Harney to General Crook, and were dated 1854 to 1877. Blue Horse had been, as he claimed, a friend to the white man, for he was one of the first Sioux army scouts, and also one of the first to cross the ocean with Buffalo Bill. The old man wanted nothing so much as an audience, and the tale of his exploits served to pass the evening. Some one had brought in a cot and an armful of blankets, and I was soon asleep.

Next morning I hunted up an Indian woman to assist in a general cleaning and overhauling of the premises. My first official act was to close up the "hole in the wall", like a ticket seller's window, through which my predecessors had been wont to deal out pills and potions to a crowd of patients standing in line, and put a sign outside the door telling them to come in.

It so happened that this was the day of the "Big Issue," on which thousands of Indians scattered over a reservation a hundred miles long by fifty wide, came to the agency for a weekly or fortnightly supply of rations, and it was a veritable "Wild West" array that greeted my astonished eyes. The streets and stores were alive with a motley crowd in picturesque garb, for all wore their best on these occasions. Every road leading to the agency was filled with white-topped lumber wagons, with here and there a more primitive travois, and young men and women on ponies' backs were gaily curvetting over the hills. The Sioux belle of that period was arrayed in grass-green or bright purple calico, loaded down with beads and bangles, and sat astride a spotted pony, holding over her glossy uncovered braids and vermilion-tinted cheeks a gaily colored silk parasol.

Toward noon, the whole population moved out two or three miles to a large corral in

79

the midst of a broad prairie, where a herd of beef cattle was held in readiness by the agency cowboys. An Indian with stentorian voice, mounted on a post, announced the names of the group whose steer was to be turned loose. Next moment the flying animal was pursued by two or three swift riders with rifles across their saddles. As the cattle were turned out in quick succession, we soon had a good imitation of the old time buffalo hunt. The galloping, long-horned steers were chased madly in every direction, amid yells and whoops, the firing of guns and clouds of yellow dust, with here and there a puff of smoke and a dull report as one stumbled and fell.

The excitement was soon over, and men of each group were busy skinning the animals, dressing the meat and dividing it among the families interested. Meanwhile the older women, sack in hand, approached the commissary, where they received their regular dole of flour, bacon, coffee, and sugar. Fires were soon blazing merrily in the various temporary camps scattered over the prairie and in the creek bottoms, and after

CHAPEL OF THE HOLY CROSS, PINE RIDGE AGENCY, USED AS
HOSPITAL FOR WOUNDED INDIANS DURING THE
"GHOST DANCE WAR."

PINE RIDGE AGENCY, 1890.

dinner, horse races and dancing were features of the day. Many white sight-seers from adjoining towns were usually on hand. Before night, most of the people had set off in a cloud of dust for their distant homes.

It is no wonder that I was kept on my feet giving out medicine throughout that day, as if from a lemonade stand at a fair. It was evident that many were merely seeking an excuse to have a look at the "Indian white doctor." Most of them diagnosed their own cases and called for some particular drug or ointment; a mixture of cod liver oil and alcohol was a favorite. It surprised them that I insisted upon examining each patient and questioning him in plain Sioux — no interpreter needed! I made a record of the interesting cases and took note of the place where they were encamped, planning to visit as many as possible in their teepees before they took again to the road.

The children of the large Government boarding school were allowed to visit their parents on issue day, and when the parting moment came, there were some pathetic scenes. It was one of my routine duties to give written excuses from school when necessary on the ground of illness, and these excuses were in much demand from lonely mothers and homesick little ones. As a last resort, the mother herself would sometimes plead illness and the need of her boy or girl for a few days at home. I was of course wholly in sympathy with the policy of education for the Indian children, yet by no means hardened to the exhibition of natural feeling. I would argue the matter with the parents as tactfully as I could; but if nothing else could win the coveted paper, the grandmother was apt to be pressed into the service, and her verbal ammunition seemed inexhaustible.

Captain Sword, the dignified and intelligent head of the Indian police force, was very friendly, and soon found time to give me a great deal of information about the place and the people. He said finally:

"Kola (my friend), the people are very glad that you have come. You have begun well; we Indians are all your friends. But I fear that we are going to have trouble. I must tell you that a new religion has been

proclaimed by some Indians in the Rocky
Mountain region, and some time ago, Sitting
Bull sent several of his men to investigate.
We hear that they have come back, saying
that they saw the prophet, or Messiah, who
told them that he is God's Son whom He has
sent into the world a second time. He told
them that He had waited nearly two thousand
years for the white men to carry out His
teachings, but instead they had destroyed
helpless small nations to satisfy their own
selfish greed. Therefore He had come again,
this time as a Savior to the red people. If
they would follow His instructions exactly,
in a little while He would cause the earth
to shake and destroy all the cities of the white
man, when famine and pestilence would
come to finish the work. The Indians must
live entirely by themselves in their teepees so
that the earthquake would not harm them.
They must fast and pray and keep up a holy
or spirit dance that He taught them. He also
ordered them to give up the white man's
clothing and make shirts and dresses in the
old style.

"My friend," Sword went on, "our reservation has been free from this new teaching until the last few weeks. Quite lately this ghost dance was introduced by Slow Bull and Kicking Bear from Rosebud" — a neighboring agency. "It has been rapidly gaining converts in many of the camps. This is what the council to-day was about. The agent says that the Great Father at Washington wishes it stopped. I fear the people will not stop. I fear trouble, kola."

I listened in silence, for I was taken entirely by surprise. Shortly afterward, the agent himself, a new man and a political appointee, approached me on the same matter. "I tell you, doctor," he began, after an exchange of greetings, "I am mighty glad you came here at just this time. We have a most difficult situation to handle, but those men down in Washington don't seem to realize the facts. If I had my way, I would have had troops here before this," he declared with emphasis. "This Ghost dance craze is the worst thing that has ever taken hold of the Indian race. It is going like wild fire among the tribes, and right here and now the people are beginning to defy my authority, and my Indian police seem to be power-less. I expect every employee on the agency to do his or her best to avert an outbreak." I assured him that he might count on me. "I shall talk to you more fully on the subject as soon as you are settled," he concluded.

I began to think the situation must be serious, and decided to consult some of the educated and Christian Indians. At this juncture a policeman appeared with a note, and handed me my orders, as I supposed. But when I opened it, I read a gracefully worded welcome and invitation to a tea party at the rectory, "to celebrate," the writer said, "my birthday, and your coming to Pine Ridge." I was caught up by the wind of destiny, but at the moment my only thought was of pleasure in the prospect of soon meeting the Reverend Charles Smith Cook, the Episcopal missionary. He was a Yankton Sioux, a graduate of Trinity College and Seabury Divinity School, and I felt sure that I should find in him a congenial friend.

I looked forward to the evening with a peculiar interest. Mr. Cook was delightful, and so was his gracious young wife, who had

85

been a New York girl. She had a sweet voice and was a trained musician. They had a little boy three or four years old. Then I met several young ladies, teachers in the boarding school, and a young man or two, and finally Miss Elaine Goodale, who was not entirely a stranger, as I had read her "Apple Blossoms" in Boston, and some of her later articles on Indian education in the *Independent* and elsewhere. Miss Goodale was supervisor of Indian schools in the Dakotas and Nebraska, and she was then at Pine Ridge on a tour of inspection. She was young for such a responsible position, but appeared equal to it in mentality and experience. I thought her very dignified and reserved, but this first evening's acquaintance showed me that she was thoroughly in earnest and absolutely sincere in her work for the Indians. I might as well admit that her personality impressed me deeply. I had laid my plans carefully, and purposed to serve my race for a few years in my profession, after which I would go to some city to practice, and I had decided that it would be wise not to think of marriage for the present. I had not given due weight to the possibility of love.

Events now crowded fast upon one another. It would seem enough that I had at last realized the dream of my life — to be of some service to my people — an ambition implanted by my earlier Indian teachers and fostered by my missionary training. I was really happy in devoting myself mind and body to my hundreds of patients who left me but few leisure moments. I soon found it absolutely necessary to have some help in the dispensary, and I enlisted the aid of George Graham, a Scotch half-breed, and a simple, friendly fellow. I soon taught him to put up the common salves and ointments, the cough syrups and other mixtures which were in most frequent demand. Together we scoured the shelves from top to bottom and prepared as best we could for the issue day crowds.

After the second "Big Issue", I had another call from Captain Sword. He began, I believe, by complimenting me upon a very busy day. "Your reputation," he declared, "has already travelled the length and breadth of the reservation. You treat everybody alike, and your directions are understood by the people. No Government doctor has ever gone freely among them before. It is a new order of things. But I fear you have come at a bad time," he added seriously. "The Ghost dancers have not heeded the agent's advice and warning. They pay no attention to us policemen. The craze is spreading like a prairie fire, and the chiefs who are encouraging it do not even come to the agency. They send after their rations and remain at home. It looks bad."

"Do they really mean mischief?" I asked incredulously, for Mr. Cook and I had discussed the matter and agreed in thinking that if the attempt was not made to stop it by force, the craze would die out of itself before long.

"They say not, and that all they ask is to be let alone. They say the white man is not disturbed when he goes to church," Sword replied. "I must tell you, however, that the agent has just ordered the police to call in all Government employees with their families to the agency. This means that something is going to happen. I have heard that he will send for soldiers to come here to stop the Ghost dance. If so, there will be trouble."

As I was still too new to the situation to grasp it fully, I concluded that in any case the only thing for me to do was to apply myself diligently to my special work, and await the issue. I had arranged to give a course of simple talks on physiology and hygiene at the Government boarding school, and on the evening of my first talk, I came back to my quarters rather late, for I had been invited to join the teachers afterward in their reading circle, and had then seen Miss Goodale safe to the rectory.

I had given up two of my rooms to Colonel Lee, the census taker, and his wife, who could find no other shelter in the crowded state of the agency, and found them awaiting me.

"Well, doc," said the jolly Colonel, "I suppose you have fixed your eye on the prettiest of the school teachers by this time!"

"I should be a callous man if I hadn't," I laughed.

"That's the right spirit. And now, here's a big bundle the stage left for you. Open it up, doc; it may be some pies or Boston baked beans from your folks!"

The parcel contained a riding suit of corduroy lined with leather, and reversible, also a pair of laced riding-boots reaching to the thigh, a present from an old friend in Boston. Nothing could have been more timely, for I now spent a good part of my days and not a few nights in the saddle. I was called to the most distant parts of the reservation, and had bought a fine white horse, part Arabian, which I named "Jack Frost." When I called for George to saddle him the next morning, I was surprised to have him hesitate.

"Don't you think, doctor, you had better keep pretty close to the agency until things are a little more settled?" he asked.

"Why, George, what do you mean?"

"Well, this news that the troops have been sent for, whether it is true or not, is making a good deal of talk. No telling what some fool Indian may take it into his head to do next. Some of the white employees are not stopping at the agency, they are going right on to the railroad. I heard one man say there is going to be an Injin outbreak and he intends to get out while he can."

VII

THE GHOST DANCE WAR

A RELIGIOUS craze such as that of 1890–91 was a thing foreign to the Indian philosophy. I recalled that a hundred years before, on the overthrow of the Algonquin nations, a somewhat similar faith was evolved by the astute Delaware prophet, brother to Tecumseh. It meant that the last hope of race entity had departed, and my people were groping blindly after spiritual relief in their bewilderment and misery. I believe that the first prophets of the "Red Christ" were innocent enough and that the people generally were sincere, but there were doubtless some who went into it for self-advertisement, and who introduced new and fantastic features to attract the crowd.

The ghost dancers had gradually concentrated on the Medicine Root creek and the edge of the "Bad Lands," and they were still further isolated by a new order from the agent, calling in all those who had not adhered to the new religion. Several thousand of these "friendlies" were soon encamped on the White Clay creek, close by the agency. It was near the middle of December, with weather unusually mild for that season. The dancers held that there would be no snow so long as their rites continued.

An Indian called Little had been guilty of some minor offense on the reservation and had hitherto evaded arrest. Suddenly he appeared at the agency on an issue day, for the express purpose, as it seemed, of defying the authorities. The assembly room of the Indian police, used also as a council room, opened out of my dispensary, and on this particular morning a council was in progress. I heard some loud talking, but was too busy to pay particular attention, though my assistant had gone in to listen to the speeches. Suddenly the place was in an uproar, and George burst into the inner office, crying excitedly "Look out for yourself, friend! They are going to fight!"

93

From the Deep Woods to Civilization

I went around to see what was going on.
A crowd had gathered just outside the council room, and the police were surrounded
by wild Indians with guns and drawn
knives in their hands. "Hurry up with
them!" one shouted, while another held his
stone war-club over a policeman's head.
The attempt to arrest Little had met with
a stubborn resistance.

At this critical moment, a fine-looking
Indian in citizen's clothes faced the excited
throng, and spoke in a clear, steady, almost
sarcastic voice.

"Stop! Think! What are you going to
do? Kill these men of our own race? Then
what? Kill all these helpless white men,
women and children? And what then?
What will these brave words, brave deeds
lead to in the end? How long can you
hold out? Your country is surrounded with
a network of railroads; thousands of white
soldiers will be here within three days.
What ammunition have you? what provisions? What will become of your families?
Think, think, my brothers! this is a child's
madness."

The Ghost Dance War

It was the "friendly" chief, American Horse, and it seems to me as I recall the incident that this man's voice had almost magic power. It is likely that he saved us all from massacre, for the murder of the police, who represented the authority of the Government, would surely have been followed by a general massacre. It is a fact that those Indians who upheld the agent were in quite as much danger from their wilder brethren as were the whites, indeed it was said that the feeling against them was even stronger. Jack Red Cloud, son of the chief, thrust the muzzle of a cocked revolver almost into the face of American Horse. "It is you and your kind," he shouted, "who have brought us to this pass!" That brave man never flinched. Ignoring his rash accuser, he quietly reëntered the office; the door closed behind him; the mob dispersed, and for the moment the danger seemed over.

That evening I was surprised by a late call from American Horse, the hero of the day. His wife entered close behind him. Scarcely were they seated when my door again opened softly, and Captain Sword came in, followed by Lieutenant Thunder Bear and most of the Indian police. My little room was crowded. I handed them some tobacco, which I had always at hand for my guests, although I did not smoke myself. After a silence, the chief got up and shook hands with me ceremoniously. In a short speech, he asked my advice in the difficult situation that confronted them between the ghost dancers, men of their own blood, and the Government to which they had pledged their loyalty.

Thanks to Indian etiquette, I could allow myself two or three minutes to weigh my words before replying. I finally said, in substance: "There is only one thing for us to do and be just to both sides. We must use every means for a peaceful settlement of this difficulty. Let us be patient; let us continue to reason with the wilder element, even though some hotheads may threaten our lives. If the worst happens, however, it is our solemn duty to serve the United States Government. Let no man ever say that we were disloyal! Following

96

such a policy, dead or alive, we shall have no apology to make."

After the others had withdrawn, Sword informed me confidentially that certain young men had threatened to kill American Horse while asleep in his tent, and that his friends had prevailed upon him and his wife to ask my hospitality for a few days. I showed Mrs. American Horse to a small room that I had vacant, and soon afterward came three strokes of the office bell — the signal for me to report at the agent's office.

I found there the agent, his chief clerk, and a visiting inspector, all of whom obviously regarded the situation as serious. "You see, doctor," said the agent, "the occurrence of to-day was planned with remarkable accuracy, so that even our alert police were taken entirely by surprise and readily overpowered. What will be the sequel we can not tell, but we must be prepared for anything. I shall be glad to have your views," he added.

I told him that I still did not believe there was any widespread plot, or deliberate intention to make war upon the whites. In my own mind, I felt sure that the arrival of troops would be construed by the ghost dancers as a threat or a challenge, and would put them at once on the defensive. I was not in favor of that step; neither was Mr. Cook, who was also called into conference; but the officials evidently feared a general uprising, and argued that it was their duty to safeguard the lives of the employees and others by calling for the soldiers without more delay. Sword, Thunder Bear, and American Horse were sent for and their opinions appeared to be fully in accord with those of the agent and inspector, so the matter was given out as settled. As a matter of fact, the agent had telegraphed to Fort Robinson for troops before he made a pretense of consulting us Indians, and they were already on their way to Pine Ridge.

I scarcely knew at the time, but gradually learned afterward, that the Sioux had many grievances and causes for profound discontent, which lay back of and were more or less closely related to the ghost dance craze and the prevailing restlessness and excitement. Rations had been cut from time to time; the people were insufficiently fed, and their protests and appeals were disregarded. Never was more ruthless fraud and graft practiced upon a defenseless people than upon these poor natives by the politicians! Never were there more worthless "scraps of paper" anywhere in the world than many of the Indian treaties and Government documents! Sickness was prevalent and the death rate alarming, especially among the children. Trouble from all these causes had for some time been developing, but might have been checked by humane and conciliatory measures. The "Messiah craze" in itself was scarcely a source of danger, and one might almost as well call upon the army to suppress Billy Sunday and his hysterical followers. Other tribes than the Sioux who adopted the new religion were let alone, and the craze died a natural death in the course of a few months.

Among the leaders of the malcontents at this time were Jack Red Cloud, No Water, He Dog, Four Bears, Yellow Bear, and Kicking Bear. Friendly leaders included Ameri-

can Horse, Young Man Afraid of his Horses,
Bad Wound, Three Stars.   There was still
another set whose attitude was not clearly
defined, and among these men was Red
Cloud, the greatest of them all.   He who
had led his people so brilliantly and with
such remarkable results, both in battle and
diplomacy, was now an old man of over
seventy years, living in a frame house which
had been built for him within a half mile of
the agency.   He would come to council,
but said little or nothing.   No one knew
exactly where he stood, but it seemed that
he was broken in spirit as in body and convinced of the hopelessness of his people's
cause.

It was Red Cloud who asked the historic
question, at a great council held in the Black
Hills region with a Government commission,
and after good Bishop Whipple had finished
the invocation, "Which God is our brother
praying to now?   Is it the same God whom
they have twice deceived, when they made
treaties with us which they afterward
broke?"

Early in the morning after the attempted

Mato-wa-nahtaka, (Kicking Bear.) High Priest of the
"Messiah Craze," 1890-91.

arrest of Little, George rushed into my quarters and awakened me. "Come quick!" he shouted, "the soldiers are here!" I looked along the White Clay creek toward the little railroad town of Rushville, Nebraska, twenty-five miles away, and just as the sun rose above the knife-edged ridges black with stunted pine, I perceived a moving cloud of dust that marked the trail of the Ninth Cavalry. There was instant commotion among the camps of friendly Indians. Many women and children were coming in to the agency for refuge, evidently fearing that the dreaded soldiers might attack their villages by mistake. Some who had not heard of their impending arrival hurried to the offices to ask what it meant. I assured those who appealed to me that the troops were here only to preserve order, but their suspicions were not easily allayed.

As the cavalry came nearer, we saw that they were colored troopers, wearing buffalo overcoats and muskrat caps; the Indians with their quick wit called them "buffalo soldiers." They halted, and established their temporary camp in the open space before the agency enclosure. The news had already gone out through the length and breadth of the reservation, and the wildest rumors were in circulation. Indian scouts might be seen upon every hill top, closely watching the military encampment.

At this juncture came the startling news from Fort Yates, some two hundred and fifty miles to the north of us, that Sitting Bull had been killed by Indian police while resisting arrest, and a number of his men with him, as well as several of the police. We next heard that the remnant of his band had fled in our direction, and soon afterward, that they had been joined by Big Foot's band from the western part of Cheyenne River agency, which lay directly in their road. United States troops continued to gather at strategic points, and of course the press seized upon the opportunity to enlarge upon the strained situation and predict an "Indian uprising." The reporters were among us, and managed to secure much "news" that no one else ever heard of. Border towns were fortified and cowboys

102

and militia gathered in readiness to protect
them against the "red devils." Certain
classes of the frontier population indus-
triously fomented the excitement for what
there was in it for them, since much money
is apt to be spent at such times. As for the
poor Indians, they were quite as badly
scared as the whites and perhaps with more
reason.

General Brooke undertook negotiations
with the ghost dancers, and finally induced
them to come within reach. They camped
on a flat about a mile north of us and in full
view, while the more tractable bands were
still gathered on the south and west. The
large boarding school had locked its doors
and succeeded in holding its hundreds of
Indian children, partly for their own sakes,
and partly as hostages for the good behavior
of their fathers. At the agency were now
gathered all the government employees and
their families, except such as had taken
flight, together with traders, missionaries,
and ranchmen, army officers, and newspaper
men. It was a conglomerate population.

During this time of grave anxiety and

nervous tension, the cooler heads among us went about our business, and still refused to believe in the tragic possibility of an Indian war. It may be imagined that I was more than busy, though I had not such long distances to cover, for since many Indians accustomed to comfortable log houses were compelled to pass the winter in tents, there was even more sickness than usual. I had access and welcome to the camps of all the various groups and factions, a privilege shared by my good friend Father Jutz, the Catholic missionary, who was completely trusted by his people.

The Christmas season was fast approaching, and this is perhaps the brightest spot in the mission year. The children of the Sunday Schools, and indeed all the people, look eagerly forward to the joyous feast; barrels and boxes are received and opened, candy bags made and filled, carols practiced, and churches decorated with ropes of spicy evergreen.

Anxious to relieve the tension in every way within his power, Mr. Cook and his helpers went on with their preparations upon

even a larger scale than usual. Since all
of the branch stations had been closed and
the people called in, it was planned to keep
the Christmas tree standing in the chapel
for a week, and to distribute gifts to a
separate congregation each evening. I found
myself pressed into the service, and passed
some happy hours in the rectory. For me,
at that critical time, there was inward struggle
as well as the threat of outward conflict, and
I could not but recall what my "white
mother" had said jokingly one day, referring
to my pleasant friendships with many charming Boston girls, "I know one Sioux who has
not been conquered, and I shall not rest
till I hear of his capture!"

I had planned to enter upon my life work
unhampered by any other ties, and declared
that all my love should be vested in my
people and my profession. At last, however,
I had met a woman whose sincerity was
convincing and whose ideals seemed very
like my own. Her childhood had been
spent almost as much out of doors as mine,
on a lonely estate high up in the Berkshire
hills; her ancestry Puritan on one side,

proud Tories on the other. She had been
moved by the appeals of that wonderful
man, General Armstrong, and had gone to
Hampton as a young girl to teach the
Indians there. After three years, she undertook pioneer work in the West as teacher of a
new camp school among the wilder Sioux,
and after much travel and study of their
peculiar problems had been offered the
appointment she now held. She spoke the
Sioux language fluently and went among
the people with the utmost freedom and
confidence. Her methods of work were
very simple and direct. I do not know
what unseen hand had guided me to her
side, but on Christmas day of 1890, Elaine
Goodale and I announced our engagement.

Three days later, we learned that Big
Foot's band of ghost dancers from the
Cheyenne river reservation north of us was
approaching the agency, and that Major
Whiteside was in command of troops with
orders to intercept them.

Late that afternoon, the Seventh Cavalry
under Colonel Forsythe was called to the
saddle and rode off toward Wounded Knee

creek, eighteen miles away. Father Craft, a Catholic priest with some Indian blood, who knew Sitting Bull and his people, followed an hour or so later, and I was much inclined to go too, but my fiancée pointed out that my duty lay rather at home with our Indians, and I stayed.

The morning of December 29th was sunny and pleasant. We were all straining our ears toward Wounded Knee, and about the middle of the forenoon we distinctly heard the reports of the Hotchkiss guns. Two hours later, a rider was seen approaching at full speed, and in a few minutes he had dismounted from his exhausted horse and handed his message to General Brooke's orderly. The Indians were watching their own messenger, who ran on foot along the northern ridges and carried the news to the so-called "hostile" camp. It was said that he delivered his message at almost the same time as the mounted officer.

The resulting confusion and excitement was unmistakable. The white teepees disappeared as if by magic and soon the caravans were in motion, going toward the natural fortress of the "Bad Lands." In the "friendly" camp there was almost as much turmoil, and crowds of frightened women and children poured into the agency. Big Foot's band had been wiped out by the troops, and reprisals were naturally looked for. The enclosure was not barricaded in any way and we had but a small detachment of troops for our protection. Sentinels were placed, and machine guns trained on the various approaches.

A few hot-headed young braves fired on the sentinels and wounded two of them. The Indian police began to answer by shooting at several braves who were apparently about to set fire to some of the outlying buildings. Every married employee was seeking a place of safety for his family, the interpreter among them. Just then General Brooke ran out into the open, shouting at the top of his voice to the police: "Stop, stop! Doctor, tell them they must not fire until ordered!" I did so, as the bullets whistled by us, and the General's coolness perhaps saved all our lives, for we were in no position to repel a large attacking force. Since we did not reply, the scattered shots soon ceased, but the situation remained critical for several days and nights.

My office was full of refugees. I called one of my good friends aside and asked him to saddle my two horses and stay by them. "When general fighting begins, take them to Miss Goodale and see her to the railroad if you can," I told him. Then I went over to the rectory. Mrs. Cook refused to go without her husband, and Miss Goodale would not leave while there was a chance of being of service. The house was crowded with terrified people, most of them Christian Indians, whom our friends were doing their best to pacify.

At dusk, the Seventh Cavalry returned with their twenty-five dead and I believe thirty-four wounded, most of them by their own comrades, who had encircled the Indians, while few of the latter had guns. A majority of the thirty or more Indian wounded were women and children, including babies in arms. As there were not tents enough for all, Mr. Cook offered us the mission chapel, in which the Christmas tree still stood, for a temporary hospital. We tore out the pews and covered the floor with hay and quilts. There we laid the poor creatures side by side in rows, and the night was devoted to caring for them as best we could. Many were frightfully torn by pieces of shells, and the suffering was terrible. General Brooke placed me in charge and I had to do nearly all the work, for although the army surgeons were more than ready to help as soon as their own men had been cared for, the tortured Indians would scarcely allow a man in uniform to touch them. Mrs. Cook, Miss Goodale, and several of Mr. Cook's Indian helpers acted as volunteer nurses. In spite of all our efforts, we lost the greater part of them, but a few recovered, including several children who had lost all their relatives and who were adopted into kind Christian families.

On the day following the Wounded Knee massacre there was a blizzard, in the midst of which I was ordered out with several Indian police, to look for a policeman who was reported to have been wounded and left some two miles from the agency. We did not find him. This was the only time during the whole affair that I carried a weapon; a friend lent me a revolver which I put in my overcoat pocket, and it was lost on the ride. On the third day it cleared, and the ground was covered with an inch or two of fresh snow. We had feared that some of the Indian wounded might have been left on the field, and a number of us volunteered to go and see. I was placed in charge of the expedition of about a hundred civilians, ten or fifteen of whom were white men. We were supplied with wagons in which to convey any whom we might find still alive. Of course a photographer and several reporters were of the party.

Fully three miles from the scene of the massacre we found the body of a woman completely covered with a blanket of snow, and from this point on we found them scattered along as they had been relentlessly hunted down and slaughtered while fleeing for their lives. Some of our people discovered relatives or friends among the dead, and there was much wailing and mourning. When we reached the spot where the

Indian camp had stood, among the fragments of burned tents and other belongings we saw the frozen bodies lying close together or piled one upon another. I counted eighty bodies of men who had been in the council and who were almost as helpless as the women and babes when the deadly fire began, for nearly all their guns had been taken from them. A reckless and desperate young Indian fired the first shot when the search for weapons was well under way, and immediately the troops opened fire from all sides, killing not only unarmed men, women, and children, but their own comrades who stood opposite them, for the camp was entirely surrounded.

It took all of my nerve to keep my composure in the face of this spectacle, and of the excitement and grief of my Indian companions, nearly every one of whom was crying aloud or singing his death song. The white men became very nervous, but I set them to examining and uncovering every body to see if one were living. Although they had been lying untended in the snow and cold for two days and nights, a number had survived. Among them I found a baby of about a year old warmly wrapped and entirely unhurt. I brought her in, and she was afterward adopted and educated by an army officer. One man who was severely wounded begged me to fill his pipe. When we brought him into the chapel he was welcomed by his wife and daughters with cries of joy, but he died a day or two later.

Under a wagon I discovered an old woman, totally blind and entirely helpless. A few had managed to crawl away to some place of shelter, and we found in a log store near by several who were badly hurt and others who had died after reaching there. After we had dispatched several wagon loads to the agency, we observed groups of warriors watching us from adjacent buttes; probably friends of the victims who had come there for the same purpose as ourselves. A majority of our party, fearing an attack, insisted that some one ride back to the agency for an escort of soldiers, and as mine was the best horse, it fell to me to go. I covered the eighteen miles in quick time and was not interfered with in any way, although if the Indians had meant mischief they could easily have picked me off from any of the ravines and gulches.

All this was a severe ordeal for one who had so lately put all his faith in the Christian love and lofty ideals of the white man. Yet I passed no hasty judgment, and was thankful that I might be of some service and relieve even a small part of the suffering. An appeal published in a Boston paper brought us liberal supplies of much needed clothing, and linen for dressings. We worked on. Bishop Hare of South Dakota visited us, and was overcome by faintness when he entered his mission chapel, thus transformed into a rude hospital.

After some days of extreme tension, and weeks of anxiety, the "hostiles," so called, were at last induced to come in and submit to a general disarmament. Father Jutz, the Catholic missionary, had gone bravely among them and used all his influence toward a peaceful settlement. The troops were all recalled and took part in a grand review before General Miles, no doubt intended to impress the Indians with their superior force.

In March, all being quiet, Miss Goodale decided to send in her resignation and go East to visit her relatives, and our wedding day was set for the following June.

VIII

WAR WITH THE POLITICIANS

WHEN the most industrious and advanced Indians on the reservation, to the number of thousands, were ordered into camp within gunshot of Pine Ridge agency, they had necessarily left their homes, their live stock, and most of their household belongings unguarded. In all troubles between the two races, history tells us that the innocent and faithful Indians have been sufferers, and this case was no exception. There was much sickness from exposure, and much unavoidable sorrow and anxiety. Furthermore, the "war" being over, these loyal Indians found that their houses had been entered and pillaged, and many of their cattle and horses had disappeared.

The authorities laid all this to the door of the "hostiles," and no doubt in some cases the charge may have been true. On the other hand, this was a golden opportunity for white horse and cattle thieves in the surrounding country, and the ranch owners within a radius of a hundred miles claimed large losses also. Moreover, the Government herd of "issue cattle" was found to be greatly depleted. It was admitted that some had been killed for food by those Indians who fled in terror to the "Bad Lands," but only a limited number could be accounted for in this way, and little of the stolen property was ever found. An inspector was ordered to examine and record these "depredation claims," and Congress passed a special appropriation of one hundred thousand dollars to pay them. We shall hear more of this later.

I have tried to make it clear that there was no "Indian outbreak" in 1890–91, and that such trouble as we had may justly be charged to the dishonest politicians, who through unfit appointees first robbed the Indians, then bullied them, and finally in a panic called for troops to suppress them. From my first days at Pine Ridge, certain Indians and white people had taken every

117

occasion to whisper into my reluctant ears
the tale of wrongs, real or fancied, committed
by responsible officials on the reservation, or
by their connivance. To me these stories
were unbelievable, from the point of view of
common decency. I held that a great
government such as ours would never con-
done or permit any such practices, while
administering large trust funds and standing
in the relation of guardian to a race made
helpless by lack of education and of legal
safeguards. At that time, I had not dreamed
what American politics really is, and I had
the most exalted admiration for our noted
public men. Accordingly, I dismissed these
reports as mere gossip or the inventions of
mischief-makers.

In March of 1891 I was invited to address
the Congregational Club of Chicago, and
on my arrival in the city I found to my surprise that the press still fostered the illusion
of a general Indian uprising in the spring.
It was reported that all the towns adjoining
the Sioux reservations had organized and
were regularly drilling a home guard for
their protection. These alarmists seemed

either ignorant or forgetful of the fact that there were only about thirty thousand Sioux altogether, or perhaps six thousand men of fighting age, more than half of whom had been civilized and Christianized for a generation and had just proved their loyalty and steadfastness through a trying time. Furthermore, the leaders of the late "hostiles" were even then in confinement in Fort Sheridan. When I was approached by the reporters, I reminded them of this, and said that everything was quiet in the field, but if there were any danger from the ghost dancers, Chicago was in the most immediate peril!

Fortunately we had in the office of Commissioner of Indian Affairs at that time a sincere man, and one who was deeply in sympathy with educational and missionary work, General Morgan of Indiana. He was a lover of fair play, and throughout my fight for justice he gave me all the support within his power. As I have before intimated, I found at Pine Ridge no conveyance for the doctor's professional use, and indeed no medical equipment worthy the name. The

119

agency doctor was thrown entirely upon his own resources, without the support of colleagues, and there was no serious attempt at sanitation or preventive work. I had spent a good part of my salary, as well as funds contributed by friends for the purpose, in the purchase of suitable medical supplies and instruments. Finally, I boldly asked for a team and buggy, also a hospital for critical cases, with a trained nurse, and a house for us to live in. Somewhat to my surprise, all of these were allowed. I was ambitious to give efficient service, so far as it was possible, and I loved my work, though the field was too large and the sick were too many for one man to care for, and there were many obstacles in the way. One was the native prejudice, still strong, against the white man's medicine, and especially against any kind of surgical operation. The people were afraid of anæsthesia, and even in cases where life depended upon it, they had steadfastly refused to allow a limb to be amputated. If I so much as put on a plaster cast, I had no sooner left our temporary hospital than they took it off.

It may be of interest to tell how this prejudice was in part overcome. One day my friend Three Stars, a Christian chief, came in with his wife, who had dislocated her shoulder. "Can you help her?" he asked. "Yes," I said, "but I must first put her to sleep. You should have brought her to me last night, when it first happened," I added, "and then that would not have been necessary."

"You know best," replied Three Stars, "I leave it entirely with you." In the presence of a number of the wounded Indians, I administered a small quantity of chloroform and jerked the arm back into its socket. She came back to consciousness laughing. It appeared to them a miracle, and I was appealed to after that whenever I dressed a painful wound, to "give me some of that stuff you gave to Three Stars' wife."

Not long afterwards, I amputated the leg of a mixed blood, which had been terribly crushed, and he not only recovered perfectly but was soon able to get about with ease on the artificial limb that I procured for him. My reputation was now established. I had gained much valuable experience, and in this connection I want to express my appreciation of the kindness of several army surgeons with whom it was my pleasure to work, one of whom took my place during a six weeks' leave of absence, when I went east to be married.

I had some interesting experiences with the Indian conjurers, or "medicine men," to use the names commonly given. I would rather say, mental healer or Christian scientist of our day, for the medicine man was all of that, and further he practised massage or osteopathy, used the Turkish bath, and some useful vegetable remedies. But his main hold on the minds of the people was gained through his appeals to the spirits and his magnetic and hypnotic powers.

I was warned that these men would seriously hamper my work, but I succeeded in avoiding antagonism by a policy of friendliness. Even when brought face to face with them in the homes of my patients, I preserved a professional and brotherly attitude. I recall one occasion when a misunderstanding between the parents of a sick child had resulted in a double call. The father, who was a policeman and a good friend of mine, urgently requested me to see his child; while the frantic mother sent for the most noted of the medicine men.

"Brother," I said, when I found him already in attendance, "I am glad you got here first. I had a long way to come, and the children need immediate attention."

"I think so too," he replied, "but now that you are here, I will withdraw."

"Why so? Surely two doctors should be better than one," I retorted. "Let us consult together. In the first place, we must determine what ails the child. Then we will decide upon the treatment." He seemed pleased, and I followed up the suggestion of a consultation by offering to enter with him the sweat bath he had prepared as a means of purification before beginning his work. After that, I had no difficulty in getting his consent to my treatment of the patient, and in time he became one of my warm friends. It was not unusual for him and other conjurers to call at my office to consult me, or "borrow" my medicine.

I had some of the wounded in my care all winter. I remember one fine looking man who was severely injured; a man of ordinary strength would have succumbed, but his strength and courage were exceptional, and best of all, he had perfect faith in my ability to restore him to health. All through those months of trial, his pretty young wife was my faithful assistant. Every morning she came to see him with her baby on her back, cheering him and inspiring us both to do our best. When at last he was able to travel, they came together to say good-bye. She handed me something, carefully wrapped in paper, and asked me not to open it until they had gone. When I did so, I found that she had cut off her beautiful long braids of hair and given them to me in token of her gratitude!

I was touched by this little illustration of woman's devotion, and happy in the thought that I was soon to realize my long dream — to become a complete man! I thought of little else than the good we two could do together, and was perfectly contented with my salary of twelve hundred dollars a year.

War with the Politicians

In spite of all that I had gone through, life was not yet a serious matter to me. I had faith in every one, and accepted civilization and Christianity at their face value — a great mistake, as I was to learn later on. I had come back to my people, not to minister to their physical needs alone, but to be a missionary in every sense of the word, and as I was much struck with the loss of manliness and independence in these, the first "reservation Indians" I had ever known, I longed above all things to help them to regain their self-respect.

On June 18, 1891, I was married to Elaine Goodale in the Church of the Ascension, New York City, by the Rev. Dr. Donald. Her two sisters were bridesmaids, and I had my chum in the medical school for best man, and two Dartmouth classmates as ushers. Many well known people were present. After the wedding breakfast in her father's apartments, we went to "Sky Farm," my wife's birth-place in the beautiful Berkshire hills, where she and her sister Dora, as little girls, wrote the "Apple Blossoms" and other poems. A reception was given for us at Dorchester by Mr. and Mrs. Wood, and after attending the Wellesley College commencement, and spending a few days with my wife's family, we returned to the West by way of Montreal. At Flandreau, South Dakota, my brother John had gathered all the family and the whole band of Flandreau Sioux to welcome us. There my father had brought me home from Canada, an absolute wild Indian, only eighteen years earlier! My honored father had been dead for some years, but my brothers had arranged to have a handsome memorial to him erected and unveiled at that time.

Our new home was building when we reached Pine Ridge, and we started life together in the old barracks, while planning the finishing and furnishing of the new. It was ready for us early in the fall. I had gained permission to add an open fireplace and a few other homelike touches at my own expense. We had the chiefs and leading men to dine with us, and quite as often some of the humbler Indians and poor old women were our guests. In fact, we kept open house, and the people loved to come and

126

ELAINE GOODALE EASTMAN.

talk with us in their own tongue. My wife accompanied me on many of my trips now that I had a carriage, and was always prepared with clean clothing, bandages, and nourishing food for my needy patients.

There was nothing I called my own save my dogs and horses and my medicine bags, yet I was perfectly happy, for I had not only gained the confidence of my people, but that of the white residents, and even the border ranchmen called me in now and then. I answered every call, and have ridden forty or fifty miles in a blizzard, over dangerous roads, sometimes at night, while my young wife suffered much more than I in the anxiety with which she awaited my return. That was a bitterly cold winter, I remember, and we had only wood fires (soft wood) and no "modern conveniences"; yet we kept in perfect health. The year rolled around and our first child was born — a little girl whom we called Dora.

Meanwhile, though the troops had been recalled, we were under military agents; there were several changes, and our relations were pleasant with them all. The time

came for the small annual payment of treaty
money, and the one hundred thousand dollar
payment for depredation claims, of which I
have spoken, was also to be made by a
special disbursing agent. This payment was
not made by check, as usual, but in cash,
and I was asked to be one of the three witnesses. I told the special agent that, as I
was almost constantly occupied, it would be
impossible for me to witness the payment,
which would take several days; but he
assured me that if only one of the three were
present at a time it would be sufficient, and,
understanding my duties to be only nominal,
I consented.

I was in the office from time to time while
the payment was going on, and saw the people
sign their names, generally by mark, on the
roll which had been prepared, opposite the
amount which each was supposed to receive;
then a clerk at another desk handed each in
turn a handful of silver and bills, and he
passed out as quickly as possible. The
money was not counted out to him, and he
was given no chance to count it until he
got outside. Even then, many could not

128

count it, and did not clearly understand
how much it ought to be, while the traders
and others were close at hand to get all or
part of it without delay.

Before I knew it, I was approached by
one and another, who declared that they had
not received the full amount, and I found
that in numerous cases reliable persons had
counted the cash as soon as the payees
came out of the office. A very able white
teacher, a college graduate, counted for
several old people who were protégés of
hers; an influential native minister did the
same, and so did several others; all reported
that the amount was short from ten to fifteen
per cent. When any one brought a shortage
to the attention of the disbursing agent or
his clerk, he was curtly told that he had
made a mistake or lost some of the money.

The complaints grew louder, and other
suspicious circumstances were reported.
Within a few days it was declared that an
investigation would be ordered. The agent
who had made the payment and immediately
left the agency, being informed of the situation, came back and tried to procure affidavits

to show that it had been an honest payment. He urged me to sign, as one of the original witnesses, arguing that I had already committed myself. I refused. I said, "After all, I did not see the full amount paid to each claimant. As the payment was conducted, it was impossible for me to do so. I trusted you, therefore I allowed you to use my name, but I don't care to sign again."

The regular agent in charge of our Indians at the time was, as I have said, an army officer, with military ideas of discipline. Like myself, he had been in the field much of the time while the payment was going on, but had officially vouched for its correctness and signed all the papers, and he took his stand upon this. He remonstrated with me for my position in the matter, and did his best to avoid an investigation; but I was convinced that a gross fraud had been committed, and in my inexperience I believed that it had only to be exposed to be corrected. I determined to do all in my power to secure justice for those poor, helpless people, even though it must appear that I was careless in signing the original papers.

War with the Politicians

I added my protest to that of others, and the department sent out a Quaker, an inspector whose record was excellent and who went about the work in a direct and straightforward way. He engaged a reliable interpreter, and called in witnesses on both sides. At the end of a fortnight, he reported that about ten thousand dollars had been dishonestly withheld from the Indians. A few of the better educated and more influential, especially mixed bloods, had been paid in full, while the old and ignorant had lost as high as fifteen or twenty per cent of their money. Evidence in support of this decision was sent to Washington.

After a short interval, I learned with astonishment that the report of this trusted inspector had not been accepted by the Secretary of the Interior, who had ordered a second investigation to supersede the first. Naturally, the second investigation was a farce and quickly ended in "whitewashing" the special payment. The next step was to punish those who had testified for the Indians or tried to bring about an honest investigation in the face of official opposition. Of these, I had been perhaps the most active and outspoken.

The usual method of disciplining agency Indians in such a case is to deprive them of various privileges, possibly of rations also, and sometimes to imprison them on trivial pretexts. White men with Indian wives, and missionaries, may be ordered off the reservation as "disturbers of the peace," while with Government employees, some grounds are usually found for their dismissal from the service.

I was promptly charged with "insubordination" and other things, but my good friend, General Morgan, then Commissioner, declined to entertain the charges, and I, on my part, kept up the fight at Washington through influential friends, and made every effort to prove my case, or rather, the case of the people, for I had at no time any personal interest in the payment. The local authorities followed the usual tactics, and undertook to force a resignation by making my position at Pine Ridge intolerable. An Indian agent has almost autocratic power, and the conditions of life on an agency are

such as to make every resident largely
dependent upon his good will. We soon
found ourselves hampered in our work and
harassed by every imaginable annoyance.
My requisitions were overlooked or "forgotten," and it became difficult to secure
the necessaries of life. I would receive a
curt written order to proceed without delay
to some remote point to visit a certain alleged
patient; then, before I had covered the
distance, would be overtaken by a mounted
policeman with arbitrary orders to return
at once to the agency. On driving in rapidly
and reporting to the agent's office for details
of the supposed emergency, I might be re-
buked for overdriving the horses, and charged
with neglect of some chronic case of which I
had either never been informed, or to which
it had been physically impossible for me to
give regular attention.

This sort of thing went on for several
months, and I was finally summoned to
Washington for a personal conference. I
think I may safely say that my story was
believed by Senators Dawes and Hoar, and
by Commissioner Morgan also. I saw the

Secretary of the Interior and the President, but they were non-committal. On my return, the same inspector who had whitewashed the payment was directed to investigate the "strained relations" between the agent and myself, and my wife, who had meantime published several very frank letters in influential eastern papers, was made a party in the case.

I will not dwell upon the farcical nature of this "investigation." The inspector was almost openly against us from the start, and the upshot of the affair was that I was shortly offered a transfer. The agent could not be dislodged, and my position had become impossible. The superintendent of the boarding school, a clergyman, and one or two others who had fought on our side were also forced to leave. We had many other warm sympathizers who could not speak out without risking their livelihood.

We declined to accept the compromise, being utterly disillusioned and disgusted with these revelations of Government mismanagement in the field, and realizing the helplessness of the best-equipped Indians to secure a fair deal for their people. Later experience, both my own and that of others, has confirmed me in this view. Had it not been for strong friends in the East and on the press, and the unusual boldness and disregard of personal considerations with which we had conducted the fight, I could not have lasted a month. All other means failing, these men will not hesitate to manufacture evidence against a man's, or a woman's, personal reputation in order to attain their ends.

It was a great disappointment to us both to give up our plans of work and our first home, to which we had devoted much loving thought and most of our little means; but it seemed to us then the only thing to do. We had not the heart to begin the same thing over again elsewhere. I resigned my position in the Indian service, and removed with my family to the city of St. Paul, where I proposed to enter upon the independent practice of medicine.

IX

CIVILIZATION AS PREACHED AND PRACTISED

AFTER thirty years of exile from the land of my nativity and the home of my ancestors, I came back to Minnesota in 1893. My mother was born on the shores of Lake Harriet; my great-grandfather's village is now a part of the beautiful park system of the city of Minneapolis.

I came to St. Paul with very little money, for one can not save much out of one hundred dollars a month, and we had been compelled to sacrifice nearly all that we had spent on our little home. It was midwinter, and our baby daughter was only eight months old; but our courage was good nevertheless. I had to wait for the regular state medical examination before being admitted to practice, as Minnesota was one of the first states to pass such a law, and the examinations were searching and covered three days' time. If I remember rightly, there were some forty-five applicants who took them with me, and I was told that nearly half of them failed to pass. It was especially hard on country practitioners who had practised successfully for many years, but were weak in theory of medicine along certain lines.

Although a young couple in a strange city, we were cordially received socially, and while seriously handicapped by lack of means, we had determined to win out. I opened an office, hung out my sign, and waited for patients. It was the hardest work I had ever done! Most of the time we were forced to board for the sake of economy, and were hard put to it to meet office rent and our modest living expenses. At this period I was peculiarly tried with various temptations, by yielding to which it seemed that I could easily relieve myself from financial strain. I was persistently solicited for illegal practice, and this by persons who were not only intelligent, but apparently of good social standing. In

their fear of exposure, they were ready to go
to large expense, and were astonished when
I refused to consider anything of the sort.
A large number came to me for Indian medicine and treatment. I told them, of course,
that I had no such medicine. Again, one
of the best known "doctors" of this class
in the Northwest invited me to go into
partnership with him. Finally, a prominent
business man of St. Paul offered to back me
up financially if I would put up an "Indian
medicine" under my own name, assuring me
that there was "a fortune in it."

To be sure, I had been bitterly disappointed
in the character of the United States army
and the honor of Government officials. Still,
I had seen the better side of civilization,
and I determined that the good men and
women who had helped me should not be
betrayed. The Christ ideal might be radical,
visionary, even impractical, as judged in the
light of my later experiences; it still seemed
to me logical, and in line with most of my
Indian training. My heart was still strong,
and I had the continual inspiration of a
brave comrade at my side.

With all the rest, I was deeply regretful of the work that I had left behind. I could not help thinking that if the President knew, if the good people of this country knew, of the wrong, it would yet be righted. I had not seen half of the savagery of civilization! While I had plenty of leisure, I began to put upon paper some of my earliest recollections, with the thought that our children might some day like to read of that wilderness life. When my wife discovered what I had written, she insisted upon sending it to *St. Nicholas*. Much to my surprise, the sketches were immediately accepted and appeared during the following year. This was the beginning of my first book, "Indian Boyhood," which was not completed until several years later.

We were slowly gaining ground, when one day a stranger called on me in my office. He was, I learned, one of the field secretaries of the International Committee of Y. M. C. A., and had apparently called to discuss the feasibility of extending this movement among the Indians. After we had talked for some time, he broached the plan of putting

139

a man into the Indian field, and ended by urging me to consider taking up the work. My first thought was that it was out of the question to sacrifice my profession and practice at this juncture, when I was just getting a promising start. Then, too, I doubted my fitness for religious work. He still pressed me to accept, pointing out the far-reaching importance of this new step, and declared that they had not been able to hear of any one else of my race so well fitted to undertake it. We took the matter under consideration, and with some reluctance I agreed to organize the field if they would meantime educate a young Indian whom I would name to be my successor. I had in mind the thought that, when the man I had chosen should be graduated from the International Training School at Springfield, Massachusetts, I could again return to my practice.

I selected Arthur Tibbetts, a Sioux, who was duly graduated in three years, when I resigned in his favor. I had been unable to keep an office in St. Paul, where we made our home, but I carried my small medical case with me on all my trips, and was often appealed to by the Indians for my professional help. I traveled over a large part of the western states and in Canada, visiting the mission stations among Indians of all tribes, and organizing young men's associations wherever conditions permitted. I think I organized some forty-three associations. This gave me a fine opportunity to study Protestant missionary effort among Indians. I seriously considered the racial attitude toward God, and almost unconsciously reopened the book of my early religious training, asking myself how it was that our simple lives were so imbued with the spirit of worship, while much church-going among white and nominally Christian Indians led often to such very small results.

A new point of view came to me then and there. This latter was a machine-made religion. It was supported by money, and more money could only be asked for on the showing made; therefore too many of the workers were after quantity rather than quality of religious experience.

I was constantly meeting with groups of young men of the Sioux, Cheyennes, Crees, Ojibways, and others, in log cabins or little frame chapels, and trying to set before them in simple language the life and character of the Man Jesus. I was cordially received everywhere, and always listened to with the closest attention. Curiously enough, even among these men who were seeking light on the white man's ideals, the racial philosophy emerged from time to time.

I remember one old battle-scarred warrior who sat among the young men got up and said, in substance: "Why, we have followed this law you speak of for untold ages! We owned nothing, because everything is from Him. Food was free, land free as sunshine and rain. Who has changed all this? The white man; and yet he says he is a believer in God! He does not seem to inherit any of the traits of his Father, nor does he follow the example set by his brother Christ."

Another of the older men had attentively followed our Bible study and attended every meeting for a whole week. I finally called

upon him for his views.   After a long silence,
he said :

"I have come to the conclusion that this
Jesus was an Indian.   He was opposed to
material acquirement and to great possessions.   He was inclined to peace.   He was
as unpractical as any Indian and set no
price upon his labor of love.   These are not
the principles upon which the white man has
founded his civilization.   It is strange that
he could not rise to these simple principles
which were commonly observed among our
people."

These words put the spell of an uncomfortable silence upon our company, but it
did not appear that the old man had intended any sarcasm or unkindness, for after
a minute he added that he was glad we had
selected such an unusual character for our
model.

At the Crow agency I met a Scotchman, a
missionary of fine type, who was doing good
work.   This man told me a strange story
of his conversion.   As a young man, he had
traveled extensively in this and other countries.   He spent one winter at Manitoba,

near an Indian reservation, and there he met a young Indian who had been converted by one of his own tribesmen, and was intensely interested in the life of Christ. This young man was a constant reader in his Indian Bible, and he talked of Christ so eloquently and so movingly as to cause serious thought on the part of the traveler. To make a long story short, he finally went home to Scotland and studied for the ministry, and then returned to America to enter the field of Indian missions. It happened that the young Indian who made so deep an impression on his white friend was my own uncle, who had been baptized Joseph Eastman.

My two uncles who were in the Custer fight lived in Canada from the time of our flight in 1862, and both died there. I was happy to be sent to that part of the country in time to see the elder one alive. He had been a father to me up to the age of fifteen, and I had not seen him for over twenty years. I found him a farmer, living in a Christian community. I had sent word in advance of my coming, and my uncle's

family had made of it a great occasion. All
of my old playmates were there. My uncle
was so happy that tears welled up in his
eyes. "When we are old," he smiled, "our
hearts are not strong in moments like this.
The Great Spirit has been kind to let me
see my boy again before I die." The early
days were recalled as we feasted together,
and all agreed that the chances were I
should have been killed before reaching the
age of twenty, if I had remained among
them; for, said they, I was very anxious
to emulate my uncle, who had been a warrior
of great reputation. Afterward I visited the
grave of my grandmother, whose devotion
had meant so much to me as a motherless
child. This was one of the great moments
of my life.

Throughout this period of my work I was
happy, being unhampered by official red
tape in the effort to improve conditions
among my people. The Superintendent of
Indian Affairs in Manitoba was very kind
and gave me every facility to go among the
Indians. He asked me to make a compara-
tive report on their condition on both sides

of the border, but this I declined to undertake, unwilling to prejudice the Government officials under whom I must carry on my work in the United States.

Another trip took me among the Ojibways, who used to take many a Sioux scalp, while we prized an eagle feather earned in battle with them. But those who had actually engaged in warlike exploits were now old and much inclined toward a peaceful life. I met some very able native preachers among them. I also visited for the first time the "Five Civilized Tribes" of the Indian Territory, now the state of Oklahoma. As is well known, these people intermarried largely among the whites, and had their own governments, schools, and thriving towns. When I appeared at Tahlequah, the Cherokee capital, the Senate took a recess in honor of their Sioux visitor. At Bacone College I addressed the students, and at the Cherokee male and female seminaries. It was an odd coincidence that at the latter school I found one of the young ladies in the act of reading an essay on my wife, Elaine Goodale Eastman!

Civilization as Preached and Practised

Among other duties of my position, I was expected to make occasional speaking trips through the East to arouse interest in the work, and it thus happened that I addressed large audiences in Chicago, New York, Boston, and at Lake Mohonk. I was taken by slum and settlement workers to visit the slums and dives of the cities, which gave another shock to my ideals of "Christian civilization." Of course, I had seen something of the poorer parts of Boston during my medical course, but not at night, and not in a way to realize the horror and wretchedness of it as I did now. To be sure, I had been taught even as a child that there are always some evil minded men in every nation, and we knew well what it is to endure physical hardship, but our poor lost nothing of their self-respect and dignity. Our great men not only divided their last kettle of food with a neighbor, but if great grief should come to them, such as the death of child or wife, they would voluntarily give away their few possessions and begin life over again in token of their sorrow. We could not conceive of the extremes of luxury

147

and misery existing thus side by side, for it was common observation with us that the coarse weeds, if permitted to grow, will choke out the more delicate flowers. These things troubled me very much; yet I still held before my race the highest, and as yet unattained, ideals of the white man.

One of the strongest rebukes I ever received from an Indian for my acceptance of these ideals and philosophy was administered by an old chief of the Sac and Fox tribe in Iowa. I was invited to visit them by the churches of Toledo and Tama City, which were much concerned by the absolute refusal of this small tribe to accept civilization and Christianity. I surmise that these good people hoped to use me as an example of the benefits of education for the Indian.

I was kindly received at their village, and made, as I thought, a pretty good speech, emphasizing the necessity of educating their children, and urging their acceptance of the Christian religion. The old chief rose to answer. He was glad that I had come to visit them. He was also glad that I was apparently satisfied with the white man's religion and his civilization. As for them, he said, neither of these had seemed good to them. The white man had showed neither respect for nature nor reverence toward God, but, he thought, tried to buy God with the by-products of nature. He tried to buy his way into heaven, but he did not even know where heaven is.

"As for us," he concluded, "we shall still follow the old trail. If you should live long, and some day the Great Spirit shall permit you to visit us again, you will find us still Indians, eating with wooden spoons out of bowls of wood. I have done."

I was even more impressed a few minutes later, when one of his people handed me my pocket book containing my railway tickets and a considerable sum of money. I had not even missed it! I said to the state missionary who was at my side, "Better let these Indians alone! If I had lost my money in the streets of your Christian city, I should probably have never seen it again."

My effort was to make the Indian feel that Christianity is not at fault for the white man's sins, but rather the lack of it, and I

149

freely admitted that this nation is not Christian, but declared that the Christians in it are trying to make it so. I found the facts and the logic of them often hard to dispute, but was partly consoled by the wonderful opportunity to come into close contact with the racial mind, and to refresh my understanding of the philosophy in which I had been trained, but which had been overlaid and superseded by a college education. I do not know how much good I accomplished, but I did my best.

X

AT THE NATION'S CAPITAL

MY work for the International Committee of Young Men's Christian Associations brought me into close association with some of the best products of American civilization. I believe that such men as Richard Morse, John R. Mott, Wilbur Messer, Charles Ober and his brother, and others, have through their organization and personal influence contributed vitally to the stability and well-being of the nation. Among the men on the International Committee whom I met at this time and who gave me a strong impression of what they stood for, were Colonel John J. McCook, David Murray, Thomas Cochrane, and Cornelius Vanderbilt. I have said some hard things of American Christianity, but in these I referred to the nation as a whole and to the majority of its people, not to individual

Christians. Had I not known some such, I should long ago have gone back to the woods.

I wished very much to resume my profession of medicine, but I was as far as ever from having the capital for a start, and we had now three children. At this juncture, I was confronted by what seemed a hopeful opportunity. Some of the leading men of the Sioux, among them my own brother, Rev. John Eastman, came to me for a consultation. They argued that I was the man of their tribe best fitted to look after their interests at Washington. They had begun to realize that certain of these interests were of great importance, involving millions of dollars. Although not a lawyer, they gave me power of attorney to act for them in behalf of these claims, and to appear as their representative before the Indian Bureau, the President, and Congress.

After signing the necessary papers, I went to Washington, where I urged our rights throughout two sessions and most of a third, while during the summers I still traveled among the Sioux. I learned that scarcely

Ohiyesa the Second, at Five Years of Age, 1903.

one of our treaties with the United States
had been carried out in good faith in all of
its provisions. After the early friendship
treaties which involved no cession of land,
the first was signed in 1824. By this agree-
ment the Sioux gave up a long strip of land
lying along the west bank of the Mississippi,
and including some of northern Missouri
and eastern Iowa. Out of the proceeds,
we paid several thousand dollars to the
Iowa and Otoe Indians who inhabited this
country conjointly with us. Next came the
treaty ratified in 1837, by which we parted
with all the territory lying in the southern
part of Wisconsin, southeastern Minnesota,
and northeastern Iowa. For this vast do-
main the Government gave us a few thousand
dollars in money and goods, together with
many promises, and established for us a trust
fund of three hundred thousand dollars,
upon which interest at five per cent was to
be paid "forever." This treaty affected
only certain bands of the Sioux.

In 1851, we ceded another large tract in
Iowa and Minnesota, including some of the
best agricultural lands in the United States,

153

and for this we were to receive ten cents an acre. Two large trust funds were established for the four bands interested, on which interest at five per cent was to be paid annually for fifty years. In addition, the Government agreed to furnish schools, farmers, blacksmith shops, etc. for the civilization of the Sioux. Only nine annual payments had been made when there was failure to meet them for two successive years. Much of our game had disappeared; the people were starving; and this state of affairs, together with other frauds on the part of Government officials and Indian traders, brought on the frightful "Minnesota massacre" in 1862. After this tragedy, many of the Sioux fled into Canada, and the remnant were moved out of the state and on to a new reservation in Nebraska. Furthermore, the remaining annuities due them under the treaty were arbitrarily confiscated as a "punishment" for the uprising. It was the claim for these lost annuities, in particular, together with some minor matters, that the Indians now desired to have adjusted, and for which they sent me to the capital.

At the Nation's Capital

Now for the first time I seriously studied the machinery of government, and before I knew it, I was a lobbyist. I came to Washington with a great respect for our public men and institutions. Although I had had some disillusionizing experiences with the lower type of political henchmen on the reservations, I reasoned that it was because they were almost beyond the pale of civilization and clothed with supreme authority over a helpless and ignorant people, that they dared do the things they did. Under the very eye of the law and of society, I thought, this could scarcely be tolerated. I was confident that a fair hearing would be granted, and our wrongs corrected without undue delay. I had overmuch faith in the civilized ideal, and I was again disappointed.

I made up my mind at the start that I would keep aloof from the shyster lawyers, and indeed I did not expect to need any legal help until the matter should come before the Court of Claims, which could not be until Congress had acted upon it.

At that time — and I am told that it is much the same now — an Indian could not do business with the Department through his attorney. The officials received me courteously enough, and assured me that the matters I spoke of should be attended to, but as soon as my back was turned, they pigeonholed them. After waiting patiently, I would resort to the plan of getting one of the Massachusetts Senators, who were my friends, to ask for the papers in the case, and this was generally effective. The Bureau chiefs soon learned that I had studied our treaty agreements and had some ground for any request that I might make. Naturally enough, every Northwestern Indian who came to Washington desired to consult me, and many of them had come on account of personal grievances which I could not take up. Complaints of every description came to my ear, not from Indians alone, as some were from earnest white men and women who had served among the Indians and had come up against official graft or abuses. I could not help them much, and had to stick pretty closely to my main business.

I was soon haunted and pestered by minor

politicians and grafters, each of whom
claimed that he was the right-hand man of
this or that congressman, and that my measure could not pass unless I had the vote of
"his" man. Of course, he expected something in exchange for that vote, or rather
the promise of it. Armed with a letter of
introduction from one of my staunch eastern
senatorial friends, I would approach a legislator who was a stranger to me, in the hope
of being allowed to explain to him the pur-
port of our measure. He would listen a
while and perhaps refer me to some one else.
I would call on the man he named, and to
my disgust be met with a demand for a
liberal percentage on the whole amount to
be recovered. If I refused to listen to this
proposal, I would soon find the legislator in
question "drumming up" some objection
to the bill, and these tactics would be kept
up until we yielded, or made some sort of
compromise. My brother John was with me
in this work. He is a fine character-reader,
and would often say to me on leaving some
one's office, "Do not trust that man; he is
dishonest; he will not keep his word." I

found after many months of effort, that
political and personal feuds in Congress
persistently delayed measures which I had
looked upon as only common justice; and
two of the injured bands have not received
their dues to this day.

I appeared from time to time before both
House and Senate committees on Indian
Affairs, and a few cases I carried to the
President. In this way I have had personal
relations with four Presidents of the United
States, Harrison, Cleveland, McKinley, and
Roosevelt. At one time I appeared before
the committee of which Senator Allison of
Iowa was chairman, on the question of
allowing the Sisseton Sioux the privilege of
leasing their unused allotments to neighboring farmers, without first referring the
agreements to the Secretary of the Interior.
The point of the request was that the red
tape and long delays that seem to be in-
separable from the system, greatly handicapped friendly and honest white farmers
in their dealings with the Indians, and, as a
result, much land lay idle and unbroken.

Some one had circulated a rumor that this

measure was fathered by one of the South
Dakota senators, with the object of securing
some fine Indian lands for his constituents.
As soon as I heard of this, I asked for a hearing,
which was granted, and I told the committee
that this was the Indians' own bill. "We
desire to learn business methods," I said,
"and we can only do this by handling our
own property. You learn by experience to
manage your business. How are we Indians
to learn if you take from us the wisdom that
is born of mistakes, and leave us to suffer
the stings of robbery and deception, with
no opportunity to guard against its recur-
rence? I know that some will misuse this
privilege, and some will be defrauded, but
the experiment will be worth all it costs."
Instead of asking me further questions upon
the bill, they asked: "Where did you go to
school? Why are there not more Indians
like you?"

As I have said, nearly every Indian delegation that came to the capital in those days —
and they were many — appealed to me for
advice, and often had me go over their
business with them before presenting it.

I was sometimes with them when they had secured their hearing before the Indian Commissioner or the committees of Congress, and in this way I heard some interesting speeches. The Ojibways have much valuable pine land, aggregating millions of dollars. Congress had passed an act authorizing a special commissioner to dispose of the lumber for the Indians' benefit, but the new man had not been long in office when it appeared that he was in with large lumber interests. There was general complaint, but as usual, the Indians were only laughed at, for the official was well entrenched behind the influence of the lumber kings, and of his political party.

At last the Ojibways succeeded in bringing the matter before the House committee on Indian affairs, of which James Sherman of New York was chairman. The chief of the delegation addressed the committee somewhat as follows:

"You are very wise men, since to you this great nation entrusts the duty of making laws for the whole people. Because of this, we have trusted you, and have hitherto respected the men whom you have sent to manage our affairs. You recently sent one who was formerly of your number to sell our pines, and he is paid with our money, ten thousand dollars a year. It has been proved that he receives money from the lumber men. He has been underselling all others. We pray you take him away! Every day that you allow him to stay, much money melts away, and great forests fall in thunder!"

Many good speeches lost their effect because of the failure of the uneducated interpreter to render them intelligently, but in this instance a fine linguist interpreted for the chief, the Rev. James Gilfillan, for many years an Episcopal missionary among the Ojibways and well acquainted with their language and ways.

The old men often amused me by their shrewd comments upon our public men. "Old Tom" Beveredge was the Indians' hotel-keeper. They all knew him, and his house was the regular rendezvous. Some Sioux chiefs who had been to call on President Harrison thus characterized him:

Said Young Man Afraid of his Horses: "He is a man of the old trail; he will never make a new one!"

White Ghost said: "There is strong religious principle in him."

Then American Horse spoke up. "The missionaries tell us that a man cannot have two masters; then how can he be a religious man and a politician at the same time?"

An old chief said of President McKinley: "I never knew a white man show so much love for mother and wife." "He has a bigger heart than most white men," declared Littlefish, "and this is unfortunate for him. The white man is a man of business, and has no use for a heart."

One day, I found a number of the chiefs in the Senate gallery. They observed closely the faces and bearing of the legislators and then gave their verdict. One man they compared to a fish. Another had not the attitude of a true man; that is, he held to a pose. Senator Morgan of Alabama they called a great councillor. Senator Hoar they estimated as a patriotic and just statesman. They picked out Senator Platt of Connecticut

as being very cautious and a diplomat. They
had much difficulty in judging Senator
Tillman, but on the whole they considered
him to be a fighting man, governed by his
emotions rather than his judgment. Some
said, he is a loyal friend; others held the
reverse. Senator Turpie of Indiana they
took for a preacher, and were pleased with
his air of godliness and reverence. Senator
Frye of Maine they thought must be a rarity
among white men — honest to the core!

It was John Grass who declared that Grover
Cleveland was the bravest white chief he
had ever known. "The harder you press
him," said he, "the stronger he stands."

Theodore Roosevelt has been well known
to the Sioux for over twenty-five years,
dating from the years of his ranch life. He
was well liked by them as a rule. Spotted
Horse said of him, "While he talked, I forgot
that he was a white man."

During Mr. Roosevelt's second admin-
istration, there was much disappointment
among the Indians. They had cherished
hopes of an honest deal, but things seemed
to be worse than ever. There were more

frauds committed; and in the way of legis-
lation, the Burke bill was distinctly a back-
ward step. The Dawes bill was framed in
the interest of the Indians; the Burke bill
was for the grafters. Therefore there was
much discouragement.

I have been much interested in the point
of view of these older Indians. Our younger
element has now been so thoroughly drilled
in the motives and methods of the white
man, at the same time losing the old mother
and family training through being placed
in boarding school from six years of age on-
ward, that they have really become an
entirely different race.

During this phase of my life, I was brought
face to face with a new phase of progress
among my people of the Dakotas. Several
of their reservations were allotted in severalty
and the Indians became full citizens and
voters. As the population of these new
states was still small and scattered, the new
voters, although few in number, were of
distinct interest to the candidates for office,
and their favor was eagerly sought. In some
counties, the Indian vote held the balance of

164

power. Naturally, they looked to the best educated men of their race to explain to them the principles and platforms of the political parties.

At first they continued to get together according to old custom, calling a council and giving a preliminary feast, at which two or three steers would be killed for a barbecue. After dinner, the tribal herald called the men together to hear the candidate or his representative. I took active part in one or two campaigns; but they have now a number of able young men who expound politics to them locally.

Some persons imagine that we are still wild savages, living on the hunt or on rations; but as a matter of fact, we Sioux are now fully entrenched, for all practical purposes, in the warfare of civilized life.

XI

BACK TO THE WOODS

IN the summer of 1910, I accepted a
commission to search out and purchase
rare curios and ethnological specimens for
one of the most important collections in
the country. Very few genuine antiques
are now to be found among Indians living
on reservations, and the wilder and more
scattered bands who still treasure them cannot easily be induced to give them up. My
method was one of indirection. I would
visit for several days in a camp where I
knew, or had reason to believe, that some
of the coveted articles were to be found.
After I had talked much with the leading
men, feasted them, and made them pres-
ents, a slight hint would often result in the
chief or medicine man "presenting" me with
some object of historic or ceremonial interest,
which etiquette would not permit to be

"sold," and which a white man would probably not have been allowed to see at all.

Within the zone of railroads and automobiles there is, I believe, only one region left in which a few roving bands of North American Indians still hold civilization at bay. The great inland seas of northern Minnesota and the Province of Ontario are surrounded by almost impenetrable jungle, the immense bogs called "muskeggs" filled with tamaracks, and the higher land with Norway, white and "jack" pines, white and red cedar, poplar and birch. The land is a paradise for moose, deer and bears, as well as the smaller fur-bearers, and the glistening black waters are a congenial home for northern fish of all kinds, of which the sturgeon is king. The waterfowl breed there in countless numbers. There are blueberries and cranberries in abundance, while the staple cereal of that region, the full-flavored wild rice, is found in the inland bays by thousands of acres.

Of this miniature world of freedom and plenty a few northern Ojibways, a branch of the great Algonquin race, are the present inhabitants, living quite to themselves and almost unconscious of the bare pathos of their survival. Here the early French traders reaped their harvest, and for a century and a half the land was under the despotic rule of the Hudson Bay Company. A powerful forerunner of civilization, this company never civilized the natives, who, moreover, had heard the "Black Robe" priests say their masses under the solemn shade of the Norway pines upon their island homes, long before Lewis and Clarke crossed the continent, and before many of the prairie tribes had so much as looked upon the face of the white man. Fortunately or unfortunately, the labyrinth in which they dwell has thus far protected them far more effectually than any treaty rights could possibly do from his almost indecent enterprise.

I know of no Indians within the borders of the United States, except those of Leech, Cass and Red Lakes in Minnesota, who still sustain themselves after the old fashion by hunting, fishing and the gathering of wild rice and berries. They do, to be sure, have a trifle of annuity money from the sale of their pine lands, and now and then they sell a few trinkets. Their permanent houses are of logs or frame, but they really do not live in them except during the coldest part of the year. Even then, some of them may be found far away from their villages, trapping for furs, which may still be disposed of at convenient points along the Canadian border. They travel by canoe or on foot, as they own very few horses, and there are no roads through the forest — only narrow trails, deeply grooved in the virgin soil.

The Leech Lake Ojibways, to whom I made my first visit, appear perfectly contented and irresponsible. They have plenty to eat of the choicest wild game, wild rice and berries. The making of maple sugar is a leading industry. The largest band and by far the most interesting is that which inhabits Bear Island, plants no gardens, will have nothing to do with schools or churches, and meets annually, as of old, for the "Grand Medicine Dance," or sacred festival, invoking the protection and blessing of the "Great Mystery" for the year to come.

From the Deep Woods to Civilization

I am a Sioux, and the Ojibways were once
the fiercest of our enemies, yet I was kindly
welcomed by the principal chief, Majigabo,
who even permitted me to witness the old
rites upon their "sacred ground." This
particular spot, they told me, had been in
use for more than forty years, and the
moose-hide drum, stretched upon a cylinder
of bass-wood, was fully as venerable. The
dance-hall was about a hundred feet long,
roofed with poles and thatch. In the center
was a rude altar, and the entrance faced the
rising sun. While the ceremonies went on,
groups of young men were sitting in the
shade and gambling with primitive dice —
small carved bones shaken in a polished bowl
of bird's-eye maple.

Majigabo is one of the few Indians left
alive who has ventured to defy a great
government with a handful of savages.
Only a few years ago, Captain Wilkinson
was shot down at the head of his troop,
while advancing to frighten the Bear Islanders
into obedience. The trouble originated in
the illegal sale of whisky to the Indians.
One of the tribesmen was summoned to

Duluth as a witness, and at the close of the trial turned loose to walk home, a distance of over a hundred miles. The weather was severe and he reached his people half-starved and sick from exposure, and the next time one was summoned, he not unnaturally refused to appear. After the death of Captain Wilkinson, no further attempt was made at coercion.

"They can take everything else, but they must let me and these island people alone," the chief said to me, and I could not but sympathize with his attitude. Only last spring he refused to allow the census taker to enumerate his people.

The next man I went to see was Boggimogishig. The old war chief of the Sugar Point band was one of those who most frequently went against the Eastern Sioux, and was often successful. This good fortune was attributed largely to the influence of the sacred war club, which had been handed down through several generations of dauntless leaders. I made use of the old-time Indian etiquette, as well as of all the wit and humor at my command, to win a wel-

come, and finally obtained from the old man
the history and traditions of his people, so
far as he knew them, and even the famous
war club itself!

At Red Lake, I found the men just returned from a successful moose hunt, and
although they greeted me kindly, it appeared
that some of the older warriors, recalling
hand-to-hand scrimmages with my forbears,
were somewhat embarrassed by the presence
of a Sioux visitor. However, after I had
been properly introduced, and had conformed
with the good old customs relating to inter-
tribal meetings, I secured several things that
I had come in search of, and among them
some very old stories. It appears that a
battle was once fought between Ojibways and
Sioux near the mouth of the stream called
Battle Creek, and while the waters of the
stream ran with blood, the color was even
discernible upon the shores of the lake,
which has ever since been known as Red
Lake. It was this battle, indeed, which
finally decided the question of occupancy,
for it is said that although my people succeeded for the time in holding off the Ojib-

ways, and cast many of the bodies of their
dead enemies into the river, they lost so
heavily themselves and became so dis-
heartened that they then left forever behind
them their forest life and exchanged the
canoe and birch-bark teepee for the prairie
and the buffalo.

But it is on Rainy Lake, remote and solitary, and still further to the north and west
upon the equally lovely Lake of the Woods,
that I found the true virgin wilderness, the
final refuge, as it appears, of American big
game and primitive man. The international
line at this point is formed by the Rainy
River, lying deep in its rocky bed and
connecting the two lakes, both of which are
adorned with thousands of exquisite islands
of a gem-like freshness and beauty. The
clear, black waters have washed, ground and
polished these rocky islets into every imaginable fantastic shape and they are all
carpeted with velvety mosses in every shade
of gray and green, and canopied with fairy-
like verdure. In every direction one is
beckoned by vistas of extraordinary charm.

These aboriginal woodsmen are in type

quite distinct from the Plains Indians.
They are generally tall and well-propor-
tioned, of somewhat lighter complexion than
their brethren to the southward, and very
grave and reticent. Their homes and food
are practically those of two centuries ago,
the only change observable being that the
inconvenient blanket is for the most part
discarded and the men carry guns instead of
bows and arrows.

It was the middle of August, the time for
tying into bundles the wild rice straw, in the
great bays where nature has so plentifully
sown it. To each family belong its sheaves,
and when the tying is finished, they are apt
to linger in the neighborhood, the women
making sacks while the men hunt. A month
later comes the harvest. Two by two they
go out in canoes, one to paddle, while the
other seizes the bundle of rice straw and
strikes a few smart blows with a stick. The
ripe grain rattles into the canoe, which,
when half full, is emptied on shore, and so
on until the watery fields are cleared.

I had now to follow these family groups to
their hidden resorts, and the sweet roving

instinct of the wild took forcible hold upon
me once more. I was eager to realize for a
few perfect days the old, wild life as I knew
it in my boyhood, and I set out with an
Ojibway guide in his birch canoe, taking
with me little that belonged to the white
man, except his guns, fishing tackle, knives,
and tobacco. The guide carried some In-
dian-made maple sugar and a sack of wild
rice, a packet of black tea and a kettle, and
we had a blanket apiece. Only think of
pitching your tent upon a new island every
day in the year! Upon many a little rocky
terrace, shaded by pine and cedar trees,
hard by a tiny harbor with its fleet of birchen
canoes, the frail bark lodges stood about in
groups, looking as if they had grown there.
Before each lodge there is a fireplace, and
near at hand the women of the family may
often be seen making nets and baskets, or
cooking the simple meal.

Early in the summer mornings there is a
pleasant stir in camp, when they glide in
canoes over the placid waters, lifting their
nets full of glistening fish. Perhaps the
sturgeon net is successful; then laughter and

175

whoops of excitement break the stillness, for the king of the lake fights for his life and pulls the boat about vigorously before he is finally knocked on the head and towed into camp.

Up on Seine Bay the favorite sport was hunting the loon, which scarcely ever takes to the wing, but dives on being approached. Most people would be put to it to guess in which direction he would reappear, at a distance of from a quarter to half a mile, but these sons of nature have learned his secret. As soon as he goes under, the canoes race for a certain point, and invariably the bird comes up among them. He is greeted with derisive laughter and cheers and immediately dives again, and the maneuver is repeated until he is winded and caught. The flesh of the loon has a strong, fishy flavor, but these Indians are very fond of it. With them nothing goes to waste; all meat or fish not needed for immediate use is cut into thin strips and smoked or dried; the hoofs of deer and moose are made into trinkets, the horns into spoons or tobacco boards, and the bones pounded to boil out the fat, which is pre-

With Guide and Bark Canoe, on Rainy Lake, Ontario.

served in dried bladders or bags of pelican
skin.

At North Bay I heard of a remarkable old
woman, said to be well over ninety years of
age, the daughter of a long-time chief during
the good old days. I called at her solitary
birch-bark teepee, and found her out, but
she soon returned bent under a load of bark
for making mats, with roots and willow twigs
for dye. She was persuaded to sit for her
picture and even to tell some old stories of
her people, which she did with much vivacity.
There are less than a hundred of them left!

The name given to this ancient crone by
the lumber-jacks is shockingly irreverent. It
is told that when she was a handsome young
woman, her father the ruling chief and honored by the Hudson Bay Company, more
than one of its employees came courting after
the fashion of those days. But the daughter
of the woods could not endure the sight of a
white man, with his repulsive hairy face. It
seems that one day, when she was approached
by a bearded voyageur, she screamed and
raised her knife, so that the man fled, cursing
her. Thereafter, whenever she saw a white

man, she would innocently repeat his oath, until she came to be known among them by that name.

As we wound in and out of the island labyrinth, new beauties met us at every turn. At one time there were not less than eight moose in sight, and the deer were plentiful and fearless. As we glided through the water, the Ojibway repeated in his broken dialect some of their traditions. We passed "Massacre island," where, more than a hundred years ago, some French traders are said to have brought the "fire water" to a large village of innocent natives, thinking thus to buy their furs for a trifle. But the Indians, when crazed with liquor, rose up and killed them all instead, even a Catholic priest who was unfortunately of the party. Since that day, the spirit of the "Black Robe", who died praying, is believed to haunt the deserted island, and no Indian ever sets foot there.

Every day it became harder for me to leave the woods. Finally I took passage on a gasoline launch that plied between a lumber camp and the little city of International

Falls. The air had been dense with smoke all day because of immense forest fires on both sides of the lake. As it grew dark we entered a narrow channel between the islands, when the wind suddenly rose, and the pilot feared lest we should be blown from the only known course, for much of the lake is not charted. He swung about for the nearest islands, a cluster of three, knowing that only on one side of one of these was it possible to land. It was dark as pitch and raining hard when we were struck broad side on by a heavy wave; the windows were knocked out and all the lights extinguished.

There was nothing to do but jump and swim for it, and it seems almost a miracle that we all landed safely. There were just four of us playing Robinson Crusoe on a lovely little isle of about an acre in extent — too small to harbor any game. The boat was gone with all its freight, except a few things that drifted ashore. Here we remained for two nights and a day before we were discovered.

This accident delayed me a day or two, as I had to buy another canoe and provisions for my last plunge into the wilderness. It carried me up Seine Bay and into the Seine River. One day we came unexpectedly upon a little Indian village of neatly made bark houses in a perfect state of preservation, but to my surprise it was uninhabited. What was still stranger, I found that whoever lived there had left all their goods behind, dishes, clothing, even bundles of furs all moth-eaten and ruined. We reached there late in the afternoon, and I immediately decided to stay the night. After supper, the guide told me that a band of Indians had lived here every winter for several years, hunting for the Hudson Bay Company. One winter many of their children were attacked by a disease unknown to them, and after several had died, the people fled in terror, leaving everything behind them. This happened, he said, eleven years before. While he was talking, beside the fire we had built in the rude mud chimney of one of the deserted cabins, in the perfectly still night, it all seemed weird and mysterious. Suddenly we heard a loud scratching on the bark door, as if some hand were feeling for the latch. He stopped speaking and we looked at one another. The scratching was repeated. "Shall I open the door?" I said. I had my hand on the trigger of my Smith and Wesson. He put more sticks on the fire. When I got the door open, there stood the biggest turtle I have ever seen, raised upon his hind feet, his eyes shining, his tail defiantly lifted, as if to tell us that he was at home there and we were the intruders.

XII

THE SOUL OF THE WHITE MAN

MY last work under the auspices of the Government was the revision of the Sioux allotment rolls, including the determination of family groups, and the assignment of surnames when these were lacking. Originally, the Indians had no family names, and confusion has been worse confounded by the admission to the official rolls of vulgar nicknames, incorrect translations, and English cognomens injudiciously bestowed upon children in the various schools. Mr. Hamlin Garland and Dr. George Bird Grinnell interested themselves in this matter some years ago, and President Roosevelt foresaw the difficulties and complications in the way of land inheritance, hence my unique commission.

My method was to select from the personal names of a family, one which should be rea-

sonably short, euphonious, and easily pronounced by the white man in the vernacular;
or, failing this, a short translation in which
the essential meaning should be preserved.
All the brothers, their wives and children
were then grouped under this as a family
name, provided their consent could be obtained to the arrangement.

While fully appreciating the Indian's viewpoint, I have tried to convince him of the
sincerity of his white friends, and that conflicts between the two races have been due as
much to mutual misunderstandings as to the
selfish greed of the white man. These
children of nature once had faith in man as
well as in God. To-day, they would suspect
even their best friend. A "century of dis-
honor" and abuse of their trust has brought
them to this. Accordingly, it was rumored
among them that the revision of names was
another cunning scheme of the white man
to defraud them of the little land still left
in their possession. The older men would
sit in my office and watch my work day after
day, before being convinced that the undertaking was really intended for their benefit

and that of their heirs. Once satisfied, they were of great assistance, for some of them knew by heart the family tree of nearly every Indian in that particular band for four generations. Their memories are remarkable, and many a fact of historic interest came up in the course of our discussions.

Such names as "Young Man of whose Horses the Enemy is Afraid", "He Kills them on Horseback", and the like, while highly regarded among us, are not easily rendered into English nor pronounced in the Dakota, and aside from such troubles, I had many difficulties with questionable marriages and orphaned children whose ancestry was not clear. Then there were cases of Indian women who had married United States soldiers and the children had been taken away from the tribe in infancy, but later returned as young men and women to claim their rights in the tribal lands.

I was directed not to recognize a plurality of wives, such as still existed among a few of the older men. Old White Bull was a fine example of the old type, and I well remember his answer when I reluctantly

184

informed him that each man must choose
one wife who should bear his name.
"What!" he exclaimed, "these two women
are sisters, both of whom have been my
wives for over half a century. I know the
way of the white man; he takes women unknown to each other and to his law. These
two have been faithful to me and I have
been faithful to them. Their children are
my children and their grandchildren are
mine. We are now living together as brother
and sisters. All the people know that we
have been happy together, and nothing but
death can separate us."

This work occupied me for six years, and
gave me insight into the relationships and
intimate history of thirty thousand Sioux.

My first book, "Indian Boyhood", em-
bodying the recollections of my wild life,
appeared in 1902, and the favor with which
it was received has encouraged me to attempt
a fuller expression of our people's life from
the inside. The present is the eighth that
I have done, always with the devoted co-
operation of my wife. Although but one
book, "Wigwam Evenings", bears both our

names, we have worked together, she in the little leisure remaining to the mother of six children, and I in the intervals of lecturing and other employment. For the past twelve years our home has been in a New England college town, and our greatest personal concern the upbringing and education of our children.

None of my earlier friends who knew me well would ever have believed that I was destined to appear in the rôle of a public speaker! It may be that I shared the native gift of oratory in some degree, but I had also the Indian reticence with strangers. Perhaps the one man most responsible for this phase of my work, aside from circumstances, was Major James B. Pond of New York city, the famous lyceum manager. Soon after the publication of "Indian Boyhood", I came from South Dakota to Brooklyn by invitation of the Twentieth Century Club of that city, to address them on the Indian. Major Pond heard of this and invited me to luncheon. He had my book with him, and after a good deal of talk, he persuaded me to go on the lecture platform under his management. He took the most cordial interest in the matter, and himself prepared the copy for my first circular. His untimely death during the next summer put a damper upon my beginning; nevertheless I filled all the dates he had made for me, and finding a growing demand, I have continued in the field ever since.

My chief object has been, not to entertain, but to present the American Indian in his true character before Americans. The barbarous and atrocious character commonly attributed to him has dated from the transition period, when the strong drink, powerful temptations, and commercialism of the white man led to deep demoralization. Really it was a campaign of education on the Indian and his true place in American history.

I have been, on the whole, happily surprised to meet with so cordial a response. Again and again I have been told by recognized thinkers, "You present an entirely new viewpoint. We can never again think of the Indian as we have done before." A great psychologist wrote me after reading "The Soul of the Indian": "My God!

187

why did we not know these things sooner?"
Many of my hearers have admitted that
morality and spirituality are found to thrive
better under the simplest conditions than
in a highly organized society, and that the
virtues are more readily cultivated where the
"struggle for existence" is merely a struggle
with the forces of nature, and not with one's
fellow-men.

The philosophy of the original American
was demonstrably on a high plane, his gift
of eloquence, wit, humor and poetry is well
established; his democracy and community
life was much nearer the ideal than ours
to-day; his standard of honor and friendship
unsurpassed, and all his faults are the faults
of generous youth.

It was not until I felt that I had to a degree
established these claims, that I consented to
appear on the platform in our ancestral garb
of honor. I feel that I was a pioneer in this
new line of defense of the native American,
not so much of his rights in the land as of
his character and religion. I am glad that
the drift is now toward a better understanding, and that he is become the ac-

knowledged hero of the Boy Scouts and Camp Fire Girls, as well as of many artists, sculptors, and sincere writers.

I was invited to represent the North American Indian at the First Universal Races Congress in London, England, in 1911. It was a great privilege to attend that gathering of distinguished representatives of 53 different nationalities, come together to mutually acquaint themselves with one another's progress and racial ideals. I was entertained by some well known men, but there was little time for purely social enjoyment. What impressed me most was the perfect equality of the races, which formed the background of all the discussions. It was declared at the outset that there is no superior race, and no inferior, since individuals of all races have proved their innate capacity by their standing in the universities of the world, and it has not seldom happened that men of the undeveloped races have surpassed students of the most advanced races in scholarship and ability.

One little incident caused some of the

delegates of the Asiatic peoples to approach me with a special friendliness. I was at a committee meeting where the platform of the Congress was being drafted, and as the first paragraph was read, I noticed that the word "Christian" appeared several times. I rose and said, "While I am myself a believer in the simple principles of Christianity, we who are met here are not all of that religion, and I would suggest that we substitute a term to which we can all subscribe, since we meet here not in the name, but in the spirit of Christianity, of universal brotherhood." Several sprang up to second the motion, among them Mr. John Milholland and Dr. Felix Adler, and as I saw Mr. Edwin D. Mead of Boston near by, I began to feel more at home. I was invited by some oriental representatives present to visit them in their own country, but as I was tied up with Chautauqua engagements, I had to take the next boat for home.

A very pleasant occasion of my meeting men and women distinguished in literature, was the banquet given to Mark Twain on his seventieth birthday. Another interesting meeting was the dinner given by the Rocky Mountain Club of New York to fifteen western governors. I believe I was the only speaker there who was not a governor! When I addressed the Camp Fire Club of America, composed largely of big game hunters in all parts of the world, I began by telling them that I had slept with a grizzly bear for three months, and often eaten with him, but had never thought of giving him away. They seemed to enter into my mood; and when I went on to tell the old chief's story of the beaver woman with one hand (she had lost the other in a steel trap) and what she and her descendants did for the tribes of men and animals, as compared with the harm wrought by the too hasty builders of a frontier town, I could not ask for a more sympathetic audience.

It has been my privilege to visit nearly all sections of our country on lecture tours, including semi-tropical Florida and the Pacific coast, the great prairie states, and almost every nook and corner of picturesque New England. I have been entertained at most of our great colleges and universities, from

191

coast to coast, and had the honor of acquaintance with many famous and interesting people, among whom I might name almost at random, W. D. Howells, Hamlin Garland, Ernest Thompson Seton, Dr.George Bird Grinnell, authors; Lorado Taft, sculptor (at the unveiling of whose colossal Black Hawk I was privileged to officiate), Edwin W. Deming, Ernest Blumenschein, and other noted artists; Mme. Bloomfield Zeisler, pianist; John Hays Hammond, engineer; Presidents G. Stanley Hall, Ernest Fox Nichols, Eliot, Stryker, Harry Pratt Judson, Dr. Luther Gulick, and other noted educators; Rabbi Stephen S. Wise, several bishops, and prominent clergymen of all denominations, together with a large circle not so well known to the public, but whose society has been to me equally stimulating and delightful.

Like every one else who is more or less in the public eye, I have a large correspondence from unknown friends, and among the most inspiring letters received have been those from foreign countries, where, until the outbreak of the European war, I had not

only generous critics, but translators of
my books in France, Germany, Austria,
Bohemia, Denmark. I am frequently asked
to recommend to readers books on all phases
of Indian life and art, also to criticize such
books both in print and in manuscript.

My work for the Boy Scouts, whose program appeals to me strongly, has given me a
good deal of practice in camp management,
finally leading to the organization of summer
camps for both boys and girls on charming
Granite Lake in the hills of southern New
Hampshire, where my whole family are
enthusiastic helpers in the development of
this form of open-air education, patterned
largely upon my own early training.

From the time I first accepted the Christ
ideal it has grown upon me steadily, but I
also see more and more plainly our modern
divergence from that ideal. I confess I
have wondered much that Christianity is
not practised by the very people who vouch
for that wonderful conception of exemplary
living. It appears that they are anxious to
pass on their religion to all races of men,
but keep very little of it themselves. I have

not yet seen the meek inherit the earth, or the peacemakers receive high honor.

Why do we find so much evil and wickedness practised by the nations composed of professedly "Christian" individuals? The pages of history are full of licensed murder and the plundering of weaker and less developed peoples, and obviously the world to-day has not outgrown this system. Behind the material and intellectual splendor of our civilization, primitive savagery and cruelty and lust hold sway, undiminished, and as it seems, unheeded. When I let go of my simple, instinctive nature religion, I hoped to gain something far loftier as well as more satisfying to the reason. Alas! it is also more confusing and contradictory. The higher and spiritual life, though first in theory, is clearly secondary, if not entirely neglected, in actual practice. When I reduce civilization to its lowest terms, it becomes a system of life based upon trade. The dollar is the measure of value, and *might* still spells *right;* otherwise, why war?

Yet even in deep jungles God's own sunlight penetrates, and I stand before my own people still as an advocate of civilization. Why? First, because there is no chance for our former simple life any more; and second, because I realize that the white man's religion is not responsible for his mistakes. There is every evidence that God has given him all the light necessary by which to live in peace and good-will with his brother; and we also know that many brilliant civilizations have collapsed in physical and moral decadence. It is for us to avoid their fate if we can.

I am an Indian; and while I have learned much from civilization, for which I am grateful, I have never lost my Indian sense of right and justice. I am for development and progress along social and spiritual lines, rather than those of commerce, nationalism, or material efficiency. Nevertheless, so long as I live, I am an American.

THE END

INDEX

ADLER, DR. FELIX, 190.

Algonquin Indians, 92, 167.

Allison, Senator William B., 158.

American Horse, 78; his pacific influence, 94, 95; interview with Eastman, 96–99; 100, 162.

Anæsthesia, Indian fear of, 120; how Eastman overcame it, 121.

"Apple Blossoms", 86.

Armstrong, General, 106.

Arnold, Matthew, 72.

Arnold Arboretum, 71.

Assiniboine Indians, 4, 10.

Assiniboine River, 10.

"BAD LANDS", 93, 108.

Bad Wound, 100.

Bancroft, Edgar A., 58.

Bartlett, President, 66.

Battle Creek, 172.

Bear Island, home of Leech Lake Ojibways, 169.

Beloit College, Eastman enters, 50; life at, 51–58.

Beveredge, Old Tom, 161.

Bible, Eastman first hears reading of, 9.

Big Foot, 102, 106, 108.

"Big Issue" day at Pine Ridge Agency, 79, 80.

Blackfeet Indians, 4.

Black Hawk, 52, 56; figure of, 192.

Blue Horse, old, 78.

Blumenschein, Ernest, 192.

Boggimogishig, Ojibway war chief, 171.

Boston, Mass., Eastman's first impressions of, 64, 65; 68; a medical student in, 70, 71; charm of, 71, 72; 74, 90, 147.

Boston University, studies medicine at, 71.

Boy Scouts, 189; interest in work of, 193.

Brooke, General, negotiations with Ghost Dancers, 103; 107; efforts to maintain peace with Indians, 108; places Eastman in charge of wounded Indians, 110.

Brooklyn, N. Y., 186.

Buffalo Bill, 78.

Burke Bill, the, 164.

CAMP FIRE CLUB OF AMERICA, 191.

Camp Fire Girls, 189.

197

Index

Cass Lake, 168.
Chapin, President, 52, 56.
Cherokee Indians, 146.
Cheyenne Indians, 49, 142.
Cheyenne River Agency, 102.
Chicago, Ill., 47, 62, 63, 118, 147.
Christ, 8, 71, 142–144, 193.
Christianity, 10, 33, 57, 59, 70, 71, 85, 125, 141, 144, 148, 151, 190, 193, 194.
Church of the Ascension, New York, Eastman's marriage in, 125.
Clemens, Samuel L., "Mark Twain ", 190.
Cleveland, President Grover, 158; an Indian's opinion of, 163.
Cochrane, Thomas, 151.
Commissioner of Indian Affairs, 119.
Congregational Club of Chicago, address before the, 118.
Congress of Races. See FIRST UNIVERSAL CONGRESS OF RACES.
Congress of the United States, 155, 156, 160.
Cook, Mrs. Charles Smith, 85, 109, 110.
Cook, Rev. Charles Smith, Eastman's first meeting with, 85; 88, 98, 104, 109, 110.
Court of Claims, 155.
Craft, Father, 107.
Crazy Horse, 30.
Cree Indians, 4, 142.

Crook, General, 78.
Crow Indians, 4, 143.
Custer, General, 30, 53.

DARTMOUTH COLLEGE, Eastman enters, 61; his life and activities at, 65–70; 72; graduation at, 74.
Davenport, Ia., 15.
Dawes, Senator H. L., 133.
Dawes Bill, the, 164.
Deming, Edwin W., 192.
Devil's Lake, N. D., 9.
Donald, Rev. Dr. Winchester, Eastman married by, 125.
Dorchester, Mass., 126.
Drink evil, 9, 10, 170, 178, 187.

EASTMAN, CHARLES A., early training, 1; feeling toward tribal foes, 2; betrayal and capture of his father, 3; early cause of hatred for United States, 3; as a youth with the Sioux, 4–6; turning-point in his life, 6–8; his father's influence, 8, 9; return with his father to the United States, 9–13; a narrow escape, 11, 12; on his father's farm, 14–16; starts his schooling, 16–30; goes to Santee, 31–40; experiences at Santee, 40–50; letter from his father, 48; earns his first money, 49; progress in his studies, 49, 50; death of his father, 50;

Index

EASTMAN, CHARLES A., —
Continued
goes to Beloit College, 51;
first ride on railroad, 51;
life at Beloit, 51, 58; life
at Knox College, 58–60;
choice of a profession, 60;
starts for the East, 61;
the journey, 61–65; in
Boston, 64; at Dartmouth
College, 65–74; reflections
and ambitions, 65; pre-
pares at Kimball Union
Academy, 66, 67; enters
Dartmouth, 67; humorous
athletic incident, 67;
broadening views, 68, 69;
interest in literature and
history, 69; summer busi-
ness experiences, 69, 70;
reverence for New Eng-
land, 70; high ideals, 71;
life in Boston, 71, 74;
acquaintance with emi-
nent men, 72; lectures at
Wellesley College, 72;
views on social life, 72,
73; graduation at Dart-
mouth, 74; appointed
government physician at
Pine Ridge Agency, 74;
attends Lake Mohonk con-
ference, 75; arrival at
Pine Ridge Agency, 76;
meager accommodations,
76, 77; "Big Issue" day,
79, 80; first learns of
Ghost Dance, 82–85; an
evening with Rev. Charles
S. Cook, 85, 86; first

meeting with his future
wife, 86; busy life at the
Agency, 87; a second
warning of the Ghost
Dance, 87–89; an accept-
able present, 90; a word
of caution, 90, 91; an
exciting incident and a
brave admonition, 93–95;
advice concerning the
Ghost Dance, 96, 98; cause
of Sioux unrest, 98, 99;
anxiety at the Agency, 99,
100; arrival of the troops,
101; wild rumors and
excitement, 102, 103; preparations for Christmas,
103, 104; engagement to
Miss Goodale, 106; dis-
turbing news from the "Bad
Lands", 107, 108; trouble
narrowly averted, 108, 109;
caring for the wounded,
109, 110; search for the
wounded after the mas-
sacre, 110–114; distressing
experience and a severe
ordeal, 113, 114; quiet
restored, 114; property
losses of the Indians, 116,
117; address in Chicago,
118, 119; friendship of the
Indian Commissioner, 119;
demands for proper equip-
ment, 120; prejudice of
the Indians, 120, 121; fear
of anæsthesia and ampu-
tation and its removal, 121;
experience with "medicine
men", 122, 123; a touch-

Index

EASTMAN, CHARLES A., —
Continued
ing tribute, 124; marriage
in New York, 125; the
new home, 126; birth
of his first child, 127;
dishonesty in payment to
Indians, 128–130; pro-
test to Washington, 131;
a farcical investigation,
131; strained relations
with Indian bureau, 132,
133; summoned to Wash-
ington, 133; leaves the
Indian service, 135; re-
moves to St. Paul, Minn.,
135; warm social welcome,
137; temporary hard-
ships, 137; professional
temptations, 137, 138; disappointment in official
character, 138; regret for
abandoned work, 139; con-
tributions to *St. Nicholas*,
139; field service for Y. M.
C. A., 139–141; extended
travel, 141; reflections on
religion, 141; Indian philosophy, 142, 143; a
Scotchman's story, 143,
144; visits his uncle in
Canada, 144, 145; among
the Ojibways, 146; in
Indian Territory, 146; address at Bacone College,
146; speaking tours in the
East, 147; depressed by
poverty of the slums, 147;
visits the Sac and Fox
tribe, 148; an old chief's

rebuke, 148, 149; efforts
to Christianize the Indians,
150; association with leading men, 151; representa-
tive of Sioux tribe in
Washington, 152–165; ces-
sions by and treaties with
the Sioux, 153, 154; bad
faith of the government,
154; trials of Washington
life, 155–157; before Con-
gressional committees, 158;
relations with four Presidents, 158; arduous duties,
158–160; Indian views of
officials, 160–163; new
phase of Indian life, 164;
Indian political influence,
164, 165; search for Indian
curios and relics, 166–181;
methods of search, 166;
his reception by former
enemies, 170; witnesses
ancient ceremonies, 170;
visits Boggimogishig, 171;
the Sugar Point Ojibways,
171; with the Red Lake
Ojibways, 172; at Rainy
Lake, 173; a fine type of
Indian, 173, 174; har-
vesting wild rice, 174;
the call of the wild, 175;
hunting the loon, 176; its
curious maneuvers, 176;
an interesting aged squaw,
177; a narrow escape from
drowning, 179; the de-
serted village, 180; a
strange visitor, 181; last
work for the government,

Index

EASTMAN, CHARLES A., —
Continued
182; the Sioux allotment
rolls, 182; confusion of
Indian names, 182;
method of work, 183;
overcoming prejudice, 183;
remarkable memory of the
Indian, 184; difficulties
of the work, 184; publication of "Indian Boyhood"
in 1902, 185; "Wigwam
Evenings", 185; writing
in collaboration with Mrs.
Eastman, 185, 186; as a
public speaker, 186; enters
the lecture field, 187;
the object in view, 187;
a cordial response, 187;
an opinion of "The Soul
of the Indian", 187, 188;
the Indian's philosophy,
188; representative to the
First Universal Races Congress, London, 1911, 198;
impressions of the Con-
gress, 189; an incident
of the Congress, 190; an
invitation from the Orient,
190; at banquet to Mark
Twain, 190; unique ap-
pearance as a speaker, 191;
before the Camp Fire Club,
191; extended traveling,
191, 192; large acquaint-
ance with noted personages,
192; voluminous and in-
spiring correspondence,
192; interest in the work
of Boy Scouts, 193; camps
for boys and girls, 193;
belief in the Christ ideal,
193; views of Christianity,
193, 194; reflections on
the higher life, 194; his
stand for civilization, 195;
belief in Indian sense of
right and justice, 195; an
American to the end, 195.
Eastman, Mrs. Charles A.
See GOODALE, ELAINE.
Eastman, Dora, eldest child
of Charles A. Eastman,
127, 136.
Eastman, Rev. John, brother
of Charles A. Eastman, 40,
44; welcomes his brother
on return from his wedding,
126; 152.
Eastman, Joseph, uncle of
Charles A. Eastman, 144.
Eliot, President Charles W.,
192.
Emerson, Ralph Waldo, 72.

FIRST UNIVERSAL RACES
CONGRESS, LONDON, 1911,
189.
"Five Civilized Tribes", 146.
Flandreau, 13; Many Light-
nings forms colony at, 16;
31; death of Many
Lightnings at, 50; family
gathering in, 126.
Forbes, Major, 9, 10.
Forsythe, Colonel, 106.
Fort Robinson, 98.
Fort Sheridan, 119.
Fort Snelling, 3.
Fort Yates, 102.

Index

Four Bears, 99.
Freeman, President Alice, 72.
Frye, Senator William P., 163.

GALESBURG, ILL., 58.
Garland, Hamlin, 182, 192.
Ghost Dance, the origin of the, 83, 84; its hold on the Indians, 84; rapid spread of the, 88; 89; foreign to the Indian philosophy, 92; seat of the trouble, 93; aggravated by presence of troops, 98; its natural death, 99; negotiations with its votaries, 103.
Gilfillan, Rev. James, 161.
Goodale, Dora, 125.
Goodale, Elaine (Mrs. Charles A. Eastman), supervisor of Indian Schools, 86; first meeting with Eastman, 86; 89; ancestry and early life, 105; takes up work for Indians, 106; her engagement, 106; faithfulness to duty, 109; duties as a nurse, 110; resigns from the Indian service, 115; her marriage, 125; at "Sky Farm", 125; birth of her daughter, 127; strained relations with Indian bureau, 134; 146; literary work in collaboration with husband, 185.
Graham, George, assistant at Pine Ridge Agency, 87; cautions Eastman, 90; 93, 101.

"Grand Medicine Dance," 169.
Grass, John, his opinion of Grover Cleveland, 163.
"Great Mystery", 9, 12, 20, 24, 26, 28, 32, 40, 41, 169.
"Great Spirit", 145, 149.
Griffis, Rev. William Eliot, 71.
Grinnell, George Bird, 182, 192.
Gros Ventres Indians, 4.
Gulick, Luther Halsey, 192.

HALL, G. STANLEY, 192.
Hammond, John Hays, 192.
Hampton Institute, 106.
Hare, Bishop, 75, 114.
Harney, General, 78.
Harriet, Lake, 136.
Harrison, President Benjamin, 158, 161.
He Dog, 99.
Hemenway, Mrs., 72.
Hoar, Senator George F., 133, 162.
Hole-in-the-Hill, 32.
Homestead laws, 14.
Howells, William Dean, 192.
Hudson Bay Company, 4, 168, 177, 180.

Independent, The, 86.
Indian Affairs, Commissioner of, 119.
"Indian Boyhood", Eastman's account of his childhood and youth in, v; publication of, 185; 186.

202

Index

Indian Police at Pine Ridge Agency, 82, 85, 88, 93–97, 108, 110.

Indian sense of right and justice, Eastman's belief in, 195.

Indian Territory, 146.

International Committee of Y. M. C. A. See Y. M. C. A.

International Falls, 178.

International Training School, Springfield, Mass., 140.

Iowa Indians, 153.

"JACK FROST", Eastman's horse at Pine Ridge, 90.

Jack Red Cloud, 95, 99.

Jamestown, N. D., 13.

Jesus. See CHRIST.

Judson, H. P., 192.

Jutz, Father, 104, 114.

KICKING BEAR, 84, 99.

Kimball Union Academy, 66, 67.

Knox College, Eastman enters, 58, 59.

LAKE OF THE WOODS, 173.

Lee, Colonel, 89, 90.

Leech Láke, 168.

Lewis and Clarke expedition, 168.

Lincoln, President Abraham, 56.

Littlefish, 162.

Longfellow, Henry Wadsworth, 72.

McCLURE, S. S., 58.

McCook, Colonel John J., 151.

McKinley, President William, 158, 162.

Majigabo, Ojibway chief, 170; defies the government, 170.

Mandan Indian, 41, 42.

Manitoba, 145.

Many Lightnings, Eastman's father, 6; his conversion, 7; describes advantages of civilized life, 7, 8; returns to United States with son, 9; Bible reading, 9; his farm, 14; forms Indian colony at Flandreau, 16; sends son to school, 16, 17; his logic, 25; advice to his son, 27; his views of religion and education, 28, 29; sends son to Indian mission at Santee, 30; letter to son, 48; his death, 50.

Mark Twain. See CLEMENS, SAMUEL L.

Massacre Island, 178.

Mead, Edwin D., 190.

Medicine, Indian, 122, 123, 138, 169.

Medicine, study of, 60, 71.

Medicine Root Creek, 92.

Messer, Wilbur, 151.

Messiah of the Ghost Dance religion, 83.

Miles, General Nelson A., 114.

Milholland, John, 190.

Index

Minneapolis, Minn., 136.
Minnesota, 3, 136, 153, 167.
Minnesota Massacre, 3.
Missouri River, 4, 43, 139.
Mohonk, Lake, 75, 147.
Moody, Dwight L., 74.
Morgan, General, Commissioner of Indian Affairs, 119, 132, 133.
Morgan, Senator John T., 162.
Morse, Richard, 151.
Mott, John R., 151.
Murray, David, 151.
Music, 37.

New York, N. Y., 125, 147.
Nichols, Ernest Fox, 192.
Ninth Cavalry, 101.
North Bay, 177.
Northern Cheyenne Indians, 49.
Northfield, Mass., 74.
No Water, 99.

Ober, Charles, 151.
Occum, Samson, 65, 69.
O-hee-ye-sa, Eastman's Indian name, 16.
Ojibway Indians, 10–12, 142, 146, 160, 161, 167, 169, 170, 172, 175, 178.
Oklahoma, 146.
Old Pine Tree, 69.
Old White Bull, 184.
Otoe Indians, 153.

Painter, Professor, 75.
Parkman, Francis, 72.
Pettibone, Professor, 53.
Phillips, John S., 58.

Philosophy of the Indian, 142, 143, 188.
Pinckney, Judge Merritt, 58.
Pine Ridge Agency, S. D., 74, 76–135.
Platt, Senator O. H., 162.
Pond, James B., 186, 187.
Pontiac, 72.
Protestant, 7, 41.

Rainey, Representative, 58.
Rainy Lake, 173.
Rainy River, 173.
"Red Christ", the, 92.
Red Cloud, 100.
Red Lake, 168, 172.
Riggs, Dr. Alfred L., superintendent of Santee school, 40; introduces Eastman to school routine, 42, 43; his personality, 48; sends Eastman to Beloit College, 50; transfers Eastman to Knox College, 58; proposes that Eastman enter Dartmouth College, 61.
Rock River, 52.
Roosevelt, President Theodore, 158; Indian admiration for, 163; foresees difficulties of Indian land inheritance, 182.
Rushville, Neb., 101.

Sac and Fox Indians, 56, 148.
St. Nicholas, magazine, 139.
St. Paul, Minn., Eastman removes to, 135; residence in, 136–140.

Index

Santee, Neb., Eastman enters Indian school at, 31; life at, 31–50.

Seabury Divinity School, 85.

Sears, Major, 40.

Seine Bay, 176, 180.

Seine River, 180.

Seton, Ernest Thompson, 192.

Seventh Cavalry, 106, 109.

Shawmut Congregational Church, Boston, 71.

Sherman, James, 160.

Sioux Indians, protest of, 3; outbreak of the, 3; Eastman member of Wah'peton clan of, 4; their friends and enemies, 4; country and habits of, 4, 5; 11, 12, 25; popularity of Santee Agency with, 30; 33; Custer annihilated by, 53; settler's fear of, 56, 57; Eastman's ambition to aid, 60; curiosity regarding the, 63; 65, 68; one of first army scouts of the, 78; gay dress of a "belle" of the, 79; "Big Issue" day with, 79–81; their idea of medical treatment, 81; ghost dance war with, 82–115; grievances of, 98; frauds practised on, 99; Miss Goodale's work among, 106; Eastman's missionary efforts with, 142; 146; Eastman rep-

resentative in Washington for, 152; cessions by and treaties with, 153; bad faith of government with, 154; Eastman pleads for, 158; old chiefs of the, 161–165; Roosevelt popular with, 163; political influence of, 164, 165; famous battle with, 172; Eastman revises allotment rolls of, 182; confusion of names of, 182–185.

Sioux language, 40, 48, 49.

Sisseton Sioux. See Sioux Indians.

Sitting Bull, 30, 49, 53, 63, 83, 102, 107.

"Sky Farm", 125.

Slow Bull, 84.

"Soul of an Indian, The", 187.

South College, Beloit, 52.

Spirit-water, 29.

Spotted Horse, 163.

Stryker, M. W., 192.

Sunday, Billy, 99.

Sword, Captain, police chief at Pine Ridge, 82, 83, 87, 88, 96–98.

Taft, Lorado, 192.

Tahlequah, Ind. Ter., 146.

Tecumseh, 92.

Three Stars, 100, 121.

Thunder Bear, Lieutenant, 96, 98.

Tibbetts, Arthur, 140.

Tillman, Senator Benjamin R., 163.

Index

Trinity College, 85.
Turpie, Senator, 163.
Twentieth Century Club of
Brooklyn, 186.

VANDERBILT, CORNELIUS, 151.

WAR CLUB, SACRED, 171.
Washington, D.C., 131, 132,
133, 152, 155.
Webster, Daniel, 69.
Wellesley College, 72, 126.
Welsh, Herbert, 75.
Whipple, Bishop, 75, 100.
White Clay Creek, 93, 101.
White Ghost, 162.
Whiteside, Major, 106.
"Wigwam Evenings", 185.
Wilkinson, Captain, 170, 171.
Williamson, Dr. John P., 48.
Wise, Rabbi Stephen S., 192.

Wood, Frank, Eastman's in-
debtedness to, 71, 72;
work for, 75; Eastman
entertained by, 126.
Wood, Mrs. Frank, 71, 72,
126.
Wounded Knee Creek, 106,
107.
Wounded Knee Massacre,
110.

Y. M. C. A., Eastman under-
takes field work for, 139,
140; his work with, 151.
Yankton City, 51.
Yellow Bear, 99.
Young Man Afraid of his
Horses, 100, 162.

ZEISLER, MADAME BLOOM-
FIELD, 192.